1982

THE WILL TO BELIEVE

THE WILL TO BELIEVE

Novelists of the Nineteen-thirties

RICHARD JOHNSTONE

Oxford New York Toronto Melbourne
OXFORD UNIVERSITY PRESS
1982

Oxford University Press, Walton Street, Oxford OX2 6DP

London Glasgow New York Toronto
Delhi Bombay Calcutta Madras Karachi
Kuala Lumpur Singapore Hong Kong Tokyo
Nairobi Dar es Salaam Cape Town
Melbourne Auckland
and associate companies in
Beirut Berlin Ibadan Mexico City

British Library Cataloguing in Publication Data
Johnstone, Richard
The will to believe.
I. English literature–20th century–
History and criticism
1. Title
820.9'00912   QR473
ISBN 0-19-211779-3

Set by Western Printing Services Ltd
Printed in Hong Kong

To my parents

Preface

This is a study of six novelists of the nineteen-thirties – Edward Upward, Rex Warner, Graham Greene, Evelyn Waugh, Christopher Isherwood, and George Orwell. They are by no means the only novelists of the period worthy of consideration, but, taken together, they do form an unusually clear instance of a group of writers whose work can be examined in the context of a common background and common influences. They were all born in the first decade of the century, and into the comparatively narrow band of the upper middle class. They were educated at public school, and, with the exception of Orwell, at Oxford or Cambridge. They began publishing in the late twenties. The directions taken during the thirties may seem very different, and in many ways of course they were; Greene and Waugh to Catholicism, Upward and Warner towards Marxism, and Isherwood and Orwell along more idiosyncratic lines. But the very proximity here of Catholicism and Marxism suggests another factor binding these novelists together. They shared a profound need for something they felt had been lost from the world, something which would have to be replaced – belief. It was a need that grew out of the past they had in common, and it marked them, by the particular forms it took, as men of their time.

When events abruptly overtook the thirties, a whole decade seemed to slide rapidly into history. The reminiscences of thirties writers began to appear in print almost immediately, and have carried on doing so ever since, reinforcing the impression of an era long gone, preserved in amber. When Christopher Isherwood, the adherent of the Hindu philosophy of Vedanta, writes from California of his experiences in the nineteen-thirties, we require a leap of imagination to make the connection. And yet there is a connection. Isherwood, like his contemporaries, belongs to the thirties, and it is only by understanding the thirties that we understand him. The questions asked by writers during those years, about the function of belief and its relationship to art, continue to be important, not least because they have not yet been satisfactorily answered.

My thanks go to all those who have, at some stage in its life, read this study, and offered valuable suggestions for its improvement. In particular, I am grateful to John Rathmell, of Christ's College, Cambridge, who supervised me as a research student, and to my wife, Beth Johnstone, who encouraged me in the project from the beginning. Some of my concluding remarks first appeared, in a different form, in the *London Magazine*, and I am grateful to the Editor for permission to include them here.

Contents

Chapter 1

A Common Background

In 1934, Wyndham Lewis looked down upon a slightly but significantly younger generation, the thirties generation, and observed a
'crisis of belief'.[1] He need have looked no further than *The Waste Land*
or his own *The Childermass* (1928) to see that this state of affairs
could not be confined to a single generation. But, as Lewis recognized, for younger, middle-class writers in the nineteen-thirties, the
crisis of belief had assumed an overwhelming importance. It dominated their lives. As a group they had much else in common. Their
years until early adolescence had been spent in Edwardian security,
in a largely mythical but nevertheless potently remembered world of
order and purpose. The past was separated from the modern world by
the Great War, and there is amongst these writers a pervasive mood
of guilty regret that their youth prevented them participating in the
catastrophe. Christopher Isherwood describes his own experience of
the phenomenon in his autobiography, *Lions and Shadows*: 'Like most
of my generation, I was obsessed by a complex of terrors and longings
connected with the idea "War". "War", in this purely neurotic sense,
meant The Test. The test of your courage, of your maturity, of your
sexual prowess: "Are you really a man?"'[2] Orwell also recalled this
sense of having failed a crucial, personal test: 'As the war fell back
into the past, my particular generation, those who had been "just too
young", became conscious of the vastness of the experience they had
missed. You felt yourself a little less than a man, because you had
missed it.'[3] The war seemed the logical culmination of the world into
which they had been born, the final test of its values. Yet they
survived, to grow into adulthood and a quite different world, of
uncertainty and change, for which they were ill-prepared. In an
entry in his diary in 1921, made when he was all of eighteen, Evelyn
Waugh sighed for 'something that went out of the world in 1914, at
least for one generation'.[4]

It is a process subsequently referred to and recognized in numerous
autobiographies and reminiscences covering the period, the movement from certainty to uncertainty, from order to chaos, a movement
which the individual feels powerless to check. William Plomer, writing in 1958, best sums up this change as it affected the thirties
generation:

Looking back from a distance, I see that the First World War, at the beginning of which I was still a child, produced a deep trauma in me . . . I had been brought up in atmospheres where it was generally accepted without question that one belonged to a race that enjoyed, as if by Divine right, a moral and material superiority which gave it the leadership of the world. . . . Pervading everything was an ideal, seldom explicit, of gentlemanliness, which included such things as not boasting, not hurting other people's feelings, never letting others feel inferior, being kind to the weak, the poor, and the old, and regarding cruelty and falsehood as the greatest of evils. . . .

No child of my generation of even minimal intelligence or sensibility could have remained untroubled by what went on in France from 1914 onwards. What had it to do with peace, or loving one's neighbour, or with forgiveness of one's enemies. . . . I had known all the wishful cant about Tommy Atkins, and the Russian steam roller, and the war to end war, and making the world safe for democracy. How could we look forward with hope, with another and probably far more destructive World War in prospect? Whom and what were we to trust in?[5]

The pre-war world which Plomer evokes belonged quite specifically to gentlemen, and the loss of which these writers speak was in many ways the loss of a birthright. Despite his recognition of its superficiality, there is implicit in Plomer's recollections a kind of nostalgia for the pleasant, uncomplicated world whose instability and even rottenness were exposed by the first war. This nostalgia, never taken completely seriously by the author, may be seen in Waugh's affection for Anchorage House in *Vile Bodies* (1930), or in the romantically pre-war past of Mr Norris in Isherwood's *Mr Norris Changes Trains* (1935). It cannot, by contrast, be seen in the working class fiction of the thirties, precisely because the 'proletarian' novelists had not shared this world of privilege and certainty – only in a novel by a member of the upper-middle class, Orwell's *Coming Up for Air* (1939), is this particular kind of consciously sentimental nostalgia expressed by a hero who is also a working man.

Isherwood, Orwell, and Plomer, in defining their attitudes to the war and to the kind of life it cut short, speak not just for themselves but for their 'generation' – rarely can so many writers have felt themselves to be so much a part of a larger group, united not by political or artistic manifesto, but by birthdates. Yet this is of course an over-simplification. The term 'my generation', as it is employed here by Isherwood, Orwell and Plomer, and by their contemporaries in other contexts, means, consciously or unconsciously, my class, and those who share my background and my education. What they had lost was something that they spent many years of their lives in an effort to regain – the certainty of a specific function in an ordered world. The plaintive despair of Plomer's question, 'Whom and what were we to trust in?', recalls the feeling of helplessness with which he and his contemporaries faced their futures, and their accompanying receptiveness to whoever or whatever might offer them security and hope. An increasingly mechanized and standardized 'post-war' society seemed to deny the value and function of the individual, and writers, like many others, turned to established creeds or beliefs as the means of defining society and the individual's place in it. They were not seeking simply to subsume their personalities and their art to a cause larger than its components, but rather to reassert the strength and purpose of the individual through the medium of belief.

Communism and Catholicism were increasingly singled out in the thirties as the alternative cures for the sickness of a generation. By 1937 a new Catholic quarterly, *Arena*, could announce that 'there are only two views of life which count in the modern world – Catholicism and Marxism'.[6] Dmitry Mirsky, in his book *The Intelligentsia of Great Britain* (1935), subscribed wholeheartedly to a notion of twin orthodoxies dividing up the intellectual middle-class between them:

Catholicism more and more becomes the magnetic guide of the live bourgeoisie and intelligentsia pointing the road to the anti-communist citadel. The intelligentsia is steadily developing a desire to get free from its good old British lack of theorising and also from its new toy of subjectivism, and steadily beginning to see that only two possibilities lie before it – catholicism and communism. To which he should turn is the dilemma of many an intellectual, and many a man who is now a catholic had hovered for a while wondering whether to become a marxist or not.[7]

The Catholic apologist Christopher Dawson arrived at similar conclusions. He saw 'the conflict between Christianity and Marxism – between the Catholic Church and the Communist party – [as] the vital issue of our time. . . . It is a conflict of rival philosophies and rival doctrines regarding the very nature of man and society.'[8] George Orwell regarded himself in the thirties as standing, virtually alone, 'between the priest and the commisar',[9] and as late as 1942 still saw the poles of belief as defining the literary landscape. 'It would be putting it too crudely to say that every poet in our time must either die young, enter the Catholic Church, or join the Communist Party, but in fact the escape from the consciousness of futility is along those general lines.'[10] Communism and Catholicism were not necessarily seen as mutually exclusive, and attempts were made to relate the two, usually however by Christians who, watching their own beliefs gradually lose ground to the increasing appeal of Communism, countered hopefully with such titles as *Christianity and the Social Revolution* (1935), or *Christ and the Workers* (1938).

There were those who observed deeper links between Communism and Catholicism. Aldous Huxley, distanced by age, and Lewis Grassic Gibbon, by class, both comment upon the similarities of the faiths, in the forms in which they appealed to young, middle class writers. Anthony Beavis in *Eyeless in Gaza* (1936) remarks to his diary that there 'seems no obvious connection between the Webbs and the Soviets on the one hand and Modern Catholicism on the other. But what profound subterranean resemblances!'[11] The worldly-wise Ma Gleghorn in Gibbon's *Grey Granite* (1934) puts it rather more pungently: '*Och, this Communism stuff's not canny, I tell you, it's just a religion though the Reds say it's not . . .*'.[12] This kind of detachment is almost invariably missing from the work of those novelists whom Gibbon refers to as 'wee chaps without chins';[13] for them, the need for belief was too absorbing and too personal a matter to be treated lightly.

An exception is Cyril Connolly. Whilst his novel *The Rock Pool* (1935) takes the predicament of his generation very seriously indeed, Connolly could also adopt the satirical view. His mock review, '*From Oscar to Stalin. A Progress.* By Christian de Clavering', is based on the career, or lack of it, of Brian Howard, bright young thing and poet *manqué* who personifies in exaggerated form the character of a generation, and who makes his ritual appearance in numerous autobiographies. The sketch consists mainly of supposed quotations from the work under review. 'Stop worrying whether he loves you or not; stop wondering how you will ever make any money. Never mind whether the trousers of your new suit turn up at the bottom; leave off trying to annoy Pa. We're onto something rather big. The Workers' Revolution for the Classless Society through the Dictatorship of the Proletariat!'[14] Christian goes on to describe his progress from childhood holidays on the Riviera, to Eton and Oxford and Paris, and finally to a little bookshop near Red Lion Square, 'full of slim volumes by unfamiliar names – who were Stephen, Wystan, Cecil and Christopher? Madge? Bates? Dutt? These blunt monosyllables spoke a new kind of language to me.'[15] Significantly, the satire is directed largely against de Clavering's revolutionary enthusiasm. The alternative of Catholicism receives only an aside; he acknowledges that there 'are one or two things I've left out, the war, the slump, the general strike, and my conversion to Catholicism, because I'm so vague about dates. But I think this will remain – A Modern Pilgrimage.'[16]

Connolly's parody helps to balance the relative significance of

Communism and Catholicism in the thirties. While to varying degrees Communism and the ideal of social revolution gripped the
literary imagination, Catholicism was undoubtedly, in terms of numbers, the less popular alternative. Contemporary comment can give
the impression of Catholicism and Communism engaged in a pitched
battle for the hearts and minds of English intellectuals, but by the
middle thirties Communism was in the ascendancy. It commanded,
for a short time at least, something between the fierce loyalty or
benign approval of most young writers, and of a number of older ones
as well. Catholicism seemed what it had in effect been to English
letters for centuries – a persistent undercurrent of belief, never gaining large numbers of literary converts, but neither showing any signs
of drying up. There is however a discernible difference in attitude
between Catholic novelists of the thirties and their immediate
predecessors. Serious Catholic novelists such as Sheila Kaye-Smith,
not to mention a stable of historical novelists adopted by the staid
Catholic journal *Blackfriars*, continued to publish into the thirties, but
they avoided the confrontation of their faith with contemporary
reality by turning to the past or to a pastoral world for their subject
matter. Catholicism formed for them part of an essentially regressive
world view, a movement away from the change and complexity of
post-war society, to a simpler world in which religion was, in every
sense, right. But to a significant minority of younger novelists,
notably Graham Greene and Evelyn Waugh, Catholicism presented
itself as the cure for the illness of the times. It became for them not a
means of retreat from the modern world, but of ordering, in fiction
and in life, a specifically contemporary reality.

Communism had a wider appeal. It is true that even amongst
writers and intellectuals the influence of Marxism was far from
universal, and it is equally true that the Marxist credentials of all but a
very few writers of the period could not then and will not now stand
much examination. Nevertheless, the idea of social revolution, the
emotional belief that a new and just society could be achieved by the
defeat of capitalist oppression, was absorbed and then publicly
avowed by large numbers of poets, novelists, and literary journalists,
and such a force cannot be easily dismissed. The new articulation of
the writer's duty to take a political stand and to attempt to influence
the course of European history is discussed by Stephen Spender in his
autobiography:

> Perhaps after all, the qualities which distinguished us from the writers of
> the previous decade lay not in ourselves, but in the events to which we
> reacted. These were unemployment, economic crisis, nascent Fascism,

approaching war. . . . The older writers were reacting in the 'twenties to the exhaustion and hopelessness of a Europe in which the old regimes were falling to pieces. We were a 'new generation', but it took me some time to appreciate the meaning of this phrase. It amounted to meaning that we had begun to write in circumstances strikingly different from those of our immediate predecessors and that a consciousness of this was shown in our writing.[17]

Spender recalls the barely defined certainty of impending disaster that began to emerge in the twenties and continued with increasing force in the thirties. Repeated references to the coming war characterize the decade, from Waugh's *Vile Bodies*, published at its beginning, to Orwell's *Coming Up for Air* at the end. Comparatively fewer writers, predominantly those associated with Auden, had by the early thirties consciously linked this certainty of war with the rise of Fascism.

The Auden group's awareness of Fascism came from Germany, filtered through what Spender describes as 'the nihilism, sophistication, and primitive vitality which was so dangerously attractive in the beginning of the Weimar Republic'.[18] But with the decline of Weimar, the underlying despair became more and more apparent. Young writers, among them Auden, Spender, John Lehmann, Christopher Isherwood, and Edward Upward, were able to see at first hand the growing power of Nazism and the threat it held for the future. It was not so much an intellectual recognition, according to Isherwood, as an absorption of 'what was in the air'.[19] The exact nature of this process is more difficult to define. In December of 1931, over two years after he first went to Germany, Isherwood published an article on 'The Youth Movement in the New Germany'. He concluded, with sentimental enthusiasm, that 'German boys and girls will grow up to be real men and women whatever their party. . . . It is to be hoped that we can say as much for our own younger generation.'[20] Rather than offering any discernible political stance, the article confirms the over-riding loyalty to the concept of youth characteristic of the thirties. It is a loyalty which underpins and to a large extent motivates the political sympathies of Isherwood and other writers of the Auden group. Social revolution was attractive to these writers not least because it offered them the means of creating a new society in their own youthful image. There is no reason to doubt awareness of Fascism as one factor pushing them towards Communism, but equally important was the instinctive rapport felt by the young writer with the Communist, both fighting the battle of youth against age, healthiness against disease.

Recalling his presence in Berlin during the burning of the Reichstag, John Lehmann demonstrates that even though by 1933 his political sympathies had become more sharply defined, the urge is still, twenty years later, to describe the events of that time in emotional and sentimental language:

... the Communists were in immediate danger of arrest, exile in concentration camps and death. Their plight in hiding, their sudden disappearances never to be explained, the tales they told of the brutality that the victorious Nazis were indulging in towards their opponents in the secrecy of barracks and prisons, the ruses that had to be invented to remove them to some kind of temporary safety, the Jew-baiting, sabre-rattling, hysterical tone of the press – all this illuminated for me the hour that had struck in Europe with blinding clarity, and keyed me up to one of those rare moments of vision when I could almost have broken into prophecy. Indeed, when a broadcast by Vernon Bartlett on the new Germany was reprinted in *The Listener*, I wrote a letter in which I denied all his hopeful and comforting conclusions and said roundly that Hitler's success meant war sooner or later. . . . From that moment, it seemed to me desperately urgent to do all in one's power to help build some kind of dam against this torrent that was sweeping down towards war. . . .[21]

The prose is consciously apocalyptic, extracting the last ounce of significance, but the sentence describing the author's consequent action – 'I wrote a letter in which I . . . said roundly . . .' – stands sadly alone. Lehmann is concerned to recreate the sheer importance to him of his political recognition; the feeling of personal significance, of a vital function in the battle against the forces of evil and blind stupidity. But the final effect is rather different; the individual and the cause remain strangely separate. The central figure, Lehmann himself, seems isolated and ineffectual.

Isherwood, in his fiction of the thirties, captures more deliberately this quality of the individual caught up in the incomprehensible, overwhelmed by events:

Hippi never worries about the future. Like everyone else in Berlin, she refers continually to the political situation, but only briefly, with a conventional melancholy, as when one speaks of religion. It is quite unreal to her. She means to go to the university, travel about, have a jolly time and eventually, of course, marry. She already has a great many boyfriends. We spent a lot of time talking about them. One has a wonderful car. Another has an aeroplane. Another has fought seven duels. Another has discovered a knack of putting out street-lamps by giving them a smart kick in a certain spot. One night, on the way back from a dance, Hippi and he put out all the street-lamps in the neighbourhood.[22]

In Germany the old system and values are in the last stages of decay, yet Hippi continues to act and plan as if nothing has happened, clinging to the security of the world she knows. Only in the last few lines does the necessity for some kind of action become apparent. Here Isherwood describes the futility of action for its own sake; for many writers Marxism seemed to offer an increasingly necessary direction and purpose.

It is difficult now to recreate exactly what the Auden group of writers understood by Marxism – what they felt and imagined when they used such words as Communist, revolution, brotherhood, workers. Spender offered in 1953 a retrospective analysis of Auden's political outlook, which contains within it something of the contradictory attitudes of himself and his contemporaries:

Auden belonged more with his conscience than either with head or heart to the anti-Fascist movement of his time. He felt, as others did, that Fascism was wicked, political persecution a crime, the Spanish Republic the best cause of the first half of the twentieth century, and that unless the public could be awakened, war was inevitable. The 1930s were a perpetual state of emergency for those aware that there was an emergency. Thus Auden felt the pressure of the necessity of doing what he could to avert the war. On the other hand, he disliked politics; he was bored by meetings and still more by the spiritual conditions which meetings signify, and he must have regarded the lives and attitudes of most of the people who were also anti-Fascists as shallow and tiresome.[23]

Spender cannot have been anxious to emphasize the naivety of earlier political enthusiasms, and is at some pains to contrast Auden's sophisticated individuality with the dull mass of Communists. But against these suggestions of world-weariness in the last sentence, the passage as a whole confirms the messianic stance taken by the Auden group, their consciousness of mission and of political insight. The political stand is presented as a simple one, adopted from simple motives.

There was however a certain calculated deliberateness which coexisted with the more obvious naivety of the political attitudes of the thirties, something which becomes clearer when Spender's observations are compared with memories of Auden recorded by Cyril Connolly:

I have said that he was ruthless, and I do not mean only that he was intellectually tougher; he was uncompromising in his feelings, in his coherence of ideas with action. He was hard-edged and unmellowed, wanting the benevolence of his later years. I remember once discussing my father and my difficult relationship with him. Wystan was adamant. 'These people just batten on one, real emotional harpies, they've got to be taught a lesson. Stand up to him, make him see you don't need him any more.'[24]

The assertion by the younger generation of the inadequate values of the past required resolute action. For many writers, Marxism seemed to provide the 'coherence' between action and ideas of which Connolly speaks. Attraction to the political drama and excitement of the period was very often emotional and unconsidered, but attraction to Marxism also contained a practical, self-serving element, for it provided the individual with a framework by which he could define the world and assert his own importance within it.

One means of illuminating the literary Marxism of the thirties is to examine the connection, often observed, between the attitudes of middle-class writers to revolutionary socialism, and their attitudes to the experience of public school. The society which as young men they regarded as outworn and repressive was often represented most powerfully in their minds by the educational institutions in which the greater part of their lives had been spent. The rebelliousness of the intelligent, sensitive schoolboy was transferred in the thirties to a larger arena. There remained the excitement to be gained from being a member of a small band on the side of the right values, but there was an added excitement too – the possibility of actually winning, of overthrowing the old system and installing the new. Their concept of revolutionary violence was a schoolboyish one, calling for the elimination of unsympathetic headmasters and of uncles with questionable share portfolios. The realisation only gradually emerged that revolutionary violence was not simply purifying and abstract, but real and subject to corruption. The subsequent process of disillusionment can be seen as part of the general movement from idealism to pragmatism which took place towards the end of the thirties, beginning with the Moscow purges and culminating in the Nazi-Soviet pact. But the part played by *Realpolitik* in the abandonment by these writers of a revolutionary stance can be overestimated. More importantly, belief in social revolution failed them personally. It had held the promise of an ordered, comprehensible world. For 'revolutionary' novelists such as Edward Upward and Rex Warner, it had seemed also to provide the means by which the hero's significance and purpose could be established, in a fictional universe defined by social revolution. Yet the problems they encountered in attempting to follow such a path proved in the end insurmountable, causing Upward to abandon fiction altogether from 1938, and Warner critically to reconsider the social revolution he advocated in 1937 in his novel *The Wild Goose Chase*.

In their desire for a new society, a revolutionary society, the writers of the Auden group may well seem to have been looking forward. But in many respects they were looking back, seeking to recreate an idealized schoolboy world in adult life. They belonged to an insular, self-obsessed generation, whose very insularity masqueraded as openness. Their youthful enthusiasm, the importance placed upon friendship and camaraderie, were based on a romanticized view of school which survived well into adulthood. As Julian Symons has pointed out, Christopher Isherwood's autobiography, subtitled *An Education in the Twenties* and published in 1938 when he was thirty-four, reads as the work of a man at least ten years younger;[25] partly because, as Isherwood has since revealed, he began work on it as early as 1932.[26] The sections dealing with schooldays reek with nostalgia. The later autobiographies of Spender (1951), Lehmann (1955), and Day Lewis (1960), are equally successful at evoking the atmosphere of schooldays long gone. One reason why they record so faithfully the workings of youthful minds is that they never really escaped that youth, but carried its ideals and priorities consciously with them into the thirties, and beyond. What Cyril Connolly in 1938 dubbed 'The Theory of Permanent Adolescence'[27] – the fascination with youth and with one's own youth in particular – can be linked with the self-consciousness of this generation as a generation. Wyndham Lewis, writing in 1932, poured scorn upon what he called 'youngergenerationism', and went on to perceive a vital distinction between the similar attitudes of a young writer called Evelyn Waugh and Waugh's elder brother Alec. In 1917, Alec Waugh had precipitated a minor scandal with *The Loom of Youth*, a novel in which he tackled obliquely the subject of adolescent sexuality. 'There is little question, in fact,' Lewis wrote, 'that had Mr Alec Waugh been born a little later he would have been an even more active agent of chronologic revolutionism, and been more prominent in Youth-politics than his brother. . . . As it is, he is a sympathetic young uncle.'[28] Lewis noticed, in other words, that while the fascination for schooldays and the concept of youth were not necessarily confined to a single age-group, the tendency to develop this fascination into a 'political' stance seemed peculiar to the thirties generation. Evelyn Waugh wrote in 1929 that 'now loyalty to one's own age is the only significant loyalty remaining to us.'[29] With this article in mind, Lewis referred in passing to Evelyn Waugh as a Marxist, as though stating the obvious. In retrospect this may seem a gross miscalculation, but in linking Waugh with left-wing writers of the same generation he was making an acute judgement on the political nature of this basic loyalty to youth – it was an articulated alliance against the old, which may or may not be further manifested in a belief in revolutionary socialism:

So the 'Mysticism of Youth' provides a kind of *temporal* substitute for the old *geographical* one of 'England, Home, and Beauty'. 'Youth', in Mr Waugh's view, is in fact a sort of *temporal Fatherland*. All merely racial aggregates have become shadowy and meaningless. There is no *esprit de corps* left in our civilization, because there is no *corps* left – a corpse if you like, but no living body. The only reality is a chronological reality. . . .

Similarly a Father and his child, or a Mother and her child, of necessity they are enemies – Time-foes: the child owes allegiance, and 'loyalty', to other children.[30]

Such an allegiance begins at school.

In *Lions and Shadows* Isherwood recalls his guilty fascination, while an undergraduate at Cambridge, for the hot house atmosphere of the public school. His unpublished first novel, also entitled *Lions and Shadows*, and an extant short story are the direct result of this fascination. (The title of the short story, 'Gems of Belgian Architecture', refers to a set of cigarette cards coveted by the boys.) Written in 1927 but not published until 1966, it is interesting for the loving detail with which the school world is recreated, and for the weight which is attached to adolescent intrigues:

Dog Major and Sale were in the Upper Fourth. They had agents in the Remove. Dog Minor was in the Upper Third and he organised agents among the Juniors. People who were not afraid of Dog Major sided with Dwight, so that he had spies in all the Walks. Dwight was in the Lower Fourth and so was Griffin. People thought that there was nearly certain to be a murder.[31]

Schoolboy jargon prefigures the popular left-wing terminology of the thirties, of spies and murders and frontiers. In a well-known remark on the genesis of Auden's 'Paid on Both sides', Isherwood records the connection between the worlds of the public school and the Icelandic saga; 'the saga-world is a schoolboy world, with its feuds, its practical jokes, its dark threats conveyed in puns and riddles and understatements. "I think this day will end unluckily for some, but chiefly for those who least expect harm."'[32] The saga, like the public school, is a closed world. Actions and characters are simplified, but these same actions are of great moment, matters of life and death. This schoolboy tendency simultaneously to simplify and dramatize recurs in the attitudes of left-wing writers to the political climate of the thirties. It led to what Bernard Bergonzi has accurately described as 'a tone and rhetoric in which it was very difficult to express political convictions seriously'.[33] Just as the intrigues and day to day machinations of school life were a game and yet desperately real and important, so the contemporary political realities were important, yet also a game.

The institutionalized life of public school and its continuation at Oxford or Cambridge served to enmesh its products in a world they could never quite outgrow. In the common artistic and political aims of the writers of the Auden group in particular, the characteristic intensity of the schoolboy friendship is importantly present. Julian Symons, impatient with such pussyfooting, has referred bluntly to the thirties as the 'homosexual decade',[34] in the sense that homosexuality, rather than talent, was often the writer's real trump card. Roy Campbell, George Orwell, and Louis MacNeice have all at one time or another expressed similar views. It is highly unlikely however that heterosexual writers were kept out of print by some kind of homosexual conspiracy. That homosexuality was more prevalent in literary London during the thirties than it was before or has been since is equally unlikely, and in any case beside the point. What is the point is that social conventions in the thirties precluded all but the most oblique references to the subject. Relationships, in the left-wing language of the time, were governed by revolutionary comradeship. Times change, however, and what it was fashionable to emphasize in the nineteen-thirties was no longer fashionable in the nineteen-seventies. Both John Lehmann's autobiographical novel, *In the Purely Pagan Sense* (1976), and Christopher Isherwood's *Christopher and His Kind* (1977), make it unequivocally clear that their political beliefs in the thirties were a function of something much more important to them, their homosexuality. Perhaps by now the emphasis is too much the other way. The decade was after all rather more than a sexual hunting ground. But Isherwood and Lehmann's later work does acknowledge what was already implicit – that for them, and doubtless for others too, political and sexual motivations were difficult to separate.

The connection between the experience at public school and the development of the thirties generation is a complex one. Not only did the child father the man, but the man frequently looked back to describe his childhood in terms of later experience. This reflexive relationship between adolescence and maturity is apparent in *Lions and Shadows*, and equally apparent in the writings of Greene, Orwell, and Waugh, all of whom saw strong correlations between themselves as schoolboys and themselves as young men. This may seem far from remarkable, but what was remarkable was the strength of the correlation and the almost obsessive interest in it. For Orwell and Greene, the memories of schooldays corresponded directly to their views of themselves in the thirties. They remembered not the camaraderie of the gang, but the loneliness of the boy who is different.

Orwell has recorded the misery of his life as an assistant pupil at St. Cyprian's Preparatory School in 'Such, Such Were the Joys'. He regarded himself as an 'outcast', and his memories are dominated by disgust:

It is not easy for me to think of my schooldays without seeming to breathe in a whiff of something cold and evil-smelling – a sort of compound of sweaty stockings, dirty towels, faecal smells blowing along corridors, forks with old food between the prongs, neck-of-mutton stew, and the banging of doors of the lavatories and the echoing chamber-pots in the dormitories.[35]

This is far removed from Isherwood's romanticized memories, but the terminology is often similar, particularly when Orwell describes a near miss with the headmaster. He has been sent on an errand in the town, and has stopped illicitly at a sweet shop. On coming out of the shop, he notices a man staring at him:

There could be no doubt as to who the man was. He was a spy placed there by Sambo! [the Headmaster] I turned away unconcernedly, and then, as though my legs were doing it of their own accord, broke into a clumsy run. But when I got round the next corner I forced myself to walk again, for to run was a sign of guilt, and obviously there would be other spies posted here and there about the town. . . . It did not seem to me strange that the headmaster of a private school should dispose of an army of informers, and I did not even imagine that he would have to pay them.[36]

The young Orwell has dared to leave the known world and venture across the border, but he remains constantly under surveillance and is forced to retreat. The imagery is that frequently employed by his contemporaries in the Auden group, but Orwell is not part of a select revolutionary band – he is an outsider, without the support of friends or allies. The analogy with his position in the thirties is clear – he suffered later from the adult version of something he describes as a 'grief peculiar to childhood and not easy to convey . . . a sense of desolate loneliness and helplessness, of being locked up not only in a hostile world but in a world of good and evil where the rules were such that it was actually not possible for me to keep them'.[37] Yet these school memories of Orwell are not entirely negative. In 'Such, Such Were the Joys', he is also relating the eventual triumph of the individual integrity over the forces of oppression.

Graham Greene, like Orwell, did not belong to any literary or political group in the thirties. His Catholicism prevented subscription to the left-wing orthodoxy of the period, but his socialist instincts placed him outside conventional Catholicism. Like Orwell, his memories of schooldays confirm this self-conception. As son of the headmaster, he felt himself to be an alien, living both in his father's house and in the school which 'began just beyond my father's study, through a green baize door'.[38] Later, at thirteen, he became a boarder, forbidden to enter his home in the same building, trapped in foreign surroundings with the security of home just over the frontier. His memories too are of disgusting smells and of failure at games, of pathetic attempts to gain stature in the eyes of his schoolfellows, and of eventual acceptance of his alien condition. Greene's personal experience led him to an overall definition of childhood, not simply his own, as 'life under a dictatorship, a condition of perpetual ignominy, irresponsibility and injustice'.[39] Thus, he felt, was the pattern of civilization irrevocably set. For Greene, only Catholicism could explain such a pattern, and his own function within it.

Evelyn Waugh, despite the political opinions which separated him from the great bulk of his contemporary novelists, also felt the absorbing interest in the schoolboy world that marks him as a man of the thirties, indicating that it was not an exclusively left-wing phenomenon. In *A Handful of Dust* the hero, Anthony Last, uses the trappings of idyllic schooldays to support his adult existence:

> Morgan Le Fay had been his room since he left the night nursery. . . . He had taken nothing from the room since he had slept there, but every year added to its contents, so that it now formed a gallery representative of every phase of his adolescence – the framed picture of a dreadnought (a coloured supplement from *Chums*), all its guns spouting flame and smoke; a photographic group of his private school; a cabinet called 'the Museum' filled with the fruits of a dozen desultory hobbies, eggs, butterflies, fossils, coins. . . .[40]

Tony Last's attempt literally to preserve his childhood is a reaction to the post-war world, an attempt to create a haven of permanence in the midst of uncertainty and chaos. The entry in Waugh's diary for 1 February, 1925, captures the profound nature of this uncertainty; 'on Friday morning I received a letter from Richard Greene telling me that he is become definitely engaged with Elizabeth. It makes me sad for them because any sort of happiness or permanence seems so infinitely remote from any one of us.'[41] Against this depressing prospect, the diaries of the twenties, until Waugh's conversion to Catholicism in 1930, reveal a premature nostalgia for the excitement and purpose of school. Only towards the end of his time at Lancing did Waugh begin to feel that he and his generation were not perhaps destined for great things:

> The more I see of Lancing the more convinced I become of the fact that our generation . . . was a very exceptional one. One day I must try and work out

the many influences which contributed to this. I think that if I do I shall find that the war is directly responsible for most of us, but lately I have been fearing that we shall have left no mark upon the House.[42]

This belated fear of leaving no mark upon the House extended in the late twenties into a pervasive feeling of insignificance and futility, to be only partly arrested by the acceptance of religious faith. For Waugh, as for his hero Tony Last, the remembered schoolboy world seems to have retained strong consolatory powers, at least until the beginning of the thirties. His need for an ideal, and his discovery of it in Catholicism, can be seen as part of the desire to recapture the order, security and happiness that in all his diaries is present only in the years covering his schooldays.

In considering the importance of schooldays in the development of this generation it does not do to generalize too much. Isherwood did after all move to the left and Waugh to the right; Stephen Spender suffered miseries at his preparatory school at least equal to those suffered by Orwell, yet became one of the most enthusiastic members of the Auden group while Orwell deliberately isolated himself. It can be said, however, that the shared background of public school and the attitude of these writers towards it, invariably helps to explain their search for belief. Schooldays became a touchstone by which these writers judged and defined the experience of later life, and became too in many cases a rich source of personal mythology. For Orwell and Greene it was having escaped from a potentially warping environment, an emblem of integrity in the face of cant. For Isherwood it was a sentimentalized world, corresponding only roughly to his real schooldays, in which he was a hero on the side of truth and justice. But taken overall, the interest in schooldays reflects the attitude of these writers to reality; the mixture, often uneasy, of realism and romance. They were of a generation that had only to remember back to childhood and early adolescence to see the results of parental values in the First World War. They wished to treat their youth dispassionately, as a time when they were moulded in the expectation that they would grow up in the same world as their fathers. Instilled in them were values which did not seem to match the realities before them, and as a result they turned critically upon the past. They seemed to regard themselves as the fortunate few who had managed to break the mould into which they had been forced, and to see the public school system in its true colours. On the other hand, schooldays held a romantic fascination that all their intellectual awareness could not dispel. In his book on the thirties, which captures the literary ambience of the period, Julian Symons observes that with the 'distaste and contempt for public school standards went very often the feeling that one had had splendid times at school'.[43] For him this is confirmation of the 'idea that every attitude contains its opposite',[44] but this contradiction is not altogether surprising. Commitment to a belief, whether political or religious or something more idiosyncratic, can be seen as a means of simplifying or codifying reality; the remembered schoolboy world was also a simplified one, where positive and negative values were clearly defined, where one's position in a social hierarchy was comfortingly secure. The emotional pull towards belief and towards the school world were both based upon this need for simplification and definition. While these writers frequently employed a kind of naive Freudianism in analysing the pernicious influence of their education and upbringing, they were also revealing, often unconsciously, the desire for a comprehensible world to replace the one that had been lost, a world where the issues were clear and one knew where one stood.

The fascination with schooldays was not merely nostalgic, for in the collective past of the thirties generation lay the means by which the experience of the thirties was defined. The remembered school-boy world offered a version of immutability. In what appeared to be the social and moral disintegration of the late twenties and early thirties, it stood as the one instance within the experience of these writers of a stable society with rules and common values, in which the function and significance of the individual were established. Such immutability carries with it the half-magical quality that Isherwood instinctively felt when he likened the schoolboy world to that of the Icelandic saga. The desire for the certainty of belief, characteristic of the generation, also carries the desire for this supernatural or super-realistic quality, a quality that may variously be termed a religious sense, a spiritual sense, or simply a sense of the profound mystery of life. The need for such a spiritual sense need not lead necessarily to Christianity – what Greene and Waugh found in Roman Catholicism was discovered by Rex Warner and Edward Upward in their particular understanding of Marxism. An explanatory system such as Communism or Catholicism asserted the significance of the individual by establishing his connection with certain constant values in his society, values which in turn lay beneath the level of observable reality.

NOTES

1. *Men Without Art* (1934) p. 86.
2. *Lions and Shadows* (1938) pp. 75–6.

3. 'My Country Right or Left' (1940) *Collected Essays, Journalism and Letters*, ed Orwell and Angus (1968) Volume 1 pp. 537–8.
4. *Diaries* (1976) p. 147.
5. *At Home* (1958) pp. 119–22.
6. Martin Turnell, 'Catholics and Marxists' *Arena* 1 (October–Dec 1937) p. 161.
7. *The Intelligentsia of Great Britain*, trans Browne (1935) p. 161.
8. *Religion and the Modern State* (1938) p. 59.
9. 'Poem' (1936), included in 'Why I Write' (1946) *Essays 1* p. 5.
10. 'Review' (1942) *Essays 2* p. 240.
11. *Eyeless in Gaza* (1936) p. 566.
12. *Grey Granite* (1934) p. 131.
13. Ibid p. 57.
14. 'Where Engels Fears to Tread' (1937) *The Condemned Playground* (1945) p. 136.
15. Ibid p. 150.
16. Ibid p. 152.
17. *World Within World* (1951) p. 139.
18. Ibid p. 108.
19. Quoted in Breon Mitchell, 'W. H. Auden and Christopher Isherwood: The "German Influence"' *Oxford German Studies* 1 (1966) p. 167.
20. 'The Youth Movement in the New Germany' *Action* 1 (10.12.31) p. 18.
21. *The Whispering Gallery* (1955) pp. 210–11.
22. *Goodbye to Berlin* (1939) pp. 36–7.
23. 'W. H. Auden and His Poetry' *Atlantic Monthly* 192 (July 1953) p. 77.
24. 'Some Memories' *W. H. Auden, A Tribute* ed Spender (1974) p. 71.
25. *The Thirties* (1975) p. 35.
26. *Christopher and His Kind* (1977) p. 72.
27. *Enemies of Promise* (1938) p. 325.
28. *Doom of Youth* (1932) p. 112.
29. 'Matter-of-Fact Mothers of the New Age' *Evening Standard* (8.4.29) p. 7.
30. *Doom of Youth* p. 107.
31. *Exhumations* (1966) pp. 177–8.
32. 'Some Notes on Auden's Early Poetry' (1937) *Exhumations* p. 19.
33. *Reading the Thirties* (1978) p. 37.
34. *The Thirties* p. 40.
35. 'Such, Such Were the Joys' (1952) *Essays 4* p. 348.
36. Ibid pp. 342–3.
37. Ibid p. 334.
38. *A Sort of Life* (1971) pp. 60–1.
39. 'Fiction' *Spectator* 150 (30.6.33) p. 956.
40. *A Handful of Dust* (1934) pp. 29–30.
41. *Diaries* p. 202.
42. Ibid p. 112.
43. *The Thirties* p. 37.
44. Ibid p. 36.

Chapter 2

Fiction and Belief

It seemed for many of these novelists of the thirties that the fictional hero could avoid sacrificing his uniqueness to an oppressive society *only* with the strength provided by commitment to a belief. Evelyn Waugh saw this problem in Christian terms, claiming that the unique individual could not be recreated in fiction without *specific* acknowledgement to the omnipotence of God. He condemned his immediate predecessors, the twenties novelists, for their attempts to ignore God:

I believe that you can only leave God out by making your characters pure abstractions. Countless admirable writers, perhaps some of the best in the world, succeed in this. Henry James was the last of them. The failure of modern novelists since and including James Joyce is one of presumption and exorbitance. They are not content with the artificial figures which hitherto passed so gracefully as men and women. They try to represent the whole human mind and soul and yet omit its determining character – that of being God's creature with a defined purpose.[1]

Waugh's argument is not an easy one to grasp. He suggests that the strength of those pre-war novelists who did not specifically acknowledge God lay in their acceptance of their own limitations, their inability to present the complete man. The failure of the twenties novelists lay in their attempt to establish a complete man in a vacuum, without the defining support of faith. Waugh is writing in 1946, shortly after the publication of his first obviously Catholic novel, *Brideshead Revisited*, and there seems to be an implied verdict passed upon his fiction of the thirties. Seen in terms of these remarks, the earlier novels function almost as cautionary tales, pointing to the inevitable limitations of the hero – Adam Fenwick-Symes or Basil Seal or Tony Last – who in his search for values ignores the possibility of religious faith.

It is however difficult to take seriously Waugh's suggestion that only the consciously Christian novelist has any hope of presenting a character who is more than a 'pure abstraction'. Graham Greene, writing at about the same time, catches the spirit of Waugh's argument in more rigorous terms. He too regards James as the last writer in a tradition. For Greene, James had the advantage of working in an age and society which contained the implicit *assumption* of God's existence, the common acceptance of social values founded in what Greene calls a 'religious sense'. But 'with the death of James the religious sense was lost to the English novel, and with the religious sense went the sense of the importance of the human act':

It was as if the world of fiction had lost a dimension: the characters of such distinguished writers as Mrs Virginia Woolf and Mr E. M. Forster wandered like cardboard symbols through a world that was paper-thin. Even in one of the most materialistic of our great novelists – in Trollope – we are aware of another world against which the actions of the characters are thrown into relief. The ungainly clergyman picking his black-booted way through the mud, handling so awkwardly his umbrella, speaking of his miserable income and stumbling through a proposal of marriage, exists in a way that Mrs Woolf's Mr Ramsay never does, because we are aware that he exists not only to the woman he is addressing but also in a God's eye. His unimportance in the world of the senses is only matched by his enormous importance in another world.

The novelist, perhaps unconsciously aware of his predicament, took refuge in the subjective novel. It was as if he thought that by mining into layers of personality hitherto untouched he could unearth the secret of 'importance', but in these mining operations he lost yet another dimension. The visible world for him ceased to exist as completely as the spiritual. Mrs Dalloway walking down Regent Street was aware of the glitter of shop windows, the smooth passage of cars, the conversation of shoppers, but it was only a Regent Street seen by Mrs Dalloway that was conveyed to the reader. . . . But, we protest, Regent Street too has a right to exist; it is more real than Mrs Dalloway, and we look back with nostalgia towards the chop houses, the mean courts, the still Sunday streets of Dickens.[2]

In common with Waugh, Greene regarded the fiction of his immediate predecessors as misdirected, as an attempt to assert the significance of the individual independent of his environment and of the deep values within it. By ignoring society and retreating into the self, any possibility of access to the very spiritual values which provide significance was denied. But for Greene and for the other novelists of his generation, the 'sense of the importance of the human act' can only be achieved if the individual, and in particular the hero, acts in a recognizable world with its own significance and purpose. The hero who acts in a world *without* any idea of its purpose or spiritual values will end, like Tony Last in *A Handful of Dust*, in a world of complete absurdity.

For Greene and Waugh, this spiritual sense which had disappeared with the First World War could only be re-established by an active assertion of faith. The same idea, without of course the faith in Christianity, is present in the more pagan terminology of Rex Warner;

what was required was a new 'recognition of the mystery which must necessarily surround our life',[3] a recognition of the very importance of existence. Warner's need for a spiritual sense, for, to put it at its most prosaic, a meaning to life, focussed upon social revolution; but, as Cecil Day Lewis has pointed out, Warner was more concerned with the need for belief than with the detailed nature of the belief itself. He was, in the early thirties, 'going through an anarchic phase that had elements both of Communist and of Fascist thought, but in general was violently heterodox and anti-establishment – a kind of seismic disturbance within himself rather than a planned programme for his own life or anyone else's'.[4] He became less 'anarchic', and developed his ideas on political action through his three novels of the thirties, but Warner always remained primarily concerned with the *function* of belief as it related to the individual. This concern extended to other novelists of the thirties generation, and allowed them a curious sympathy with Christianity even while rejecting it. Warner, Upward, and Orwell regarded twentieth-century Christianity as the sad survivor of a once vigorous faith. They saw no possibility of adapting Christianity to the needs of the thirties, but were aware that it had once dictated the purposes of existence. Virtues such as courage and honesty had not been abstract humanist qualities, but soundly rooted in Christian doctrine. In this respect, Warner and Upward tended to regard Christianity as a legitimate precursor of Marxism, and their attitude was a kind of equivocal respect. Roy, the hero of Warner's *The Aerodrome* (1941), feels both contempt and sympathy for the church as it is embodied in his 'father'; he is aware of its superficiality and its hypocrisy, but at the same time he is unwilling to dismiss out of hand the values for which it claims to stand.

Edward Upward saw Christianity as a form of 'magic' which had not finally succeeded in providing a convincing explanation of the world and the individual's function within it. In *Journey to the Border*, (1938) he describes a modern curate as an 'intransigent popularizer of a reversed, a twisted picture of the world', but goes on to say that 'once – a thousand, even two hundred years ago – he would have been in the right. Then there was no real opportunity for the mass of the people to better their material conditions.'[5] Upward clearly regards past faith in Christianity as understandable in the circumstances. It was a means of establishing a 'heaven within', when there seemed no convincing prospect of changing the world without. But now, in the twentieth century, 'men had mastered nature, and the requisite conditions now existed for creating – not a heaven on earth, but a society in which every man and woman would at least have the chance to be normally happy'.[6] Yet although physical conditions are now favourable, Upward sees no possibility of achieving this state by the unaided efforts of the people; instead they will have the support of a new belief, in 'the way of the workers'. Upward does not regard the individual as capable of standing alone: he requires the support of belief in social revolution if he is to maintain his individuality. He strongly resists any simple equation of Christianity and social action in *Journey to the Border*, but their functions as he describes them are very similar. The abiding difference is that Christianity belongs to the past, whereas social revolution is the only valid object of belief in the twentieth century. The attraction towards revolutionary action springs from an instinctive need for belief, and in an interview in 1964 Upward emphasized the relative importance of the instinctive or the 'emotional' element in his commitment to Marxism: 'None of the available philosophies seemed to regard emotion as a reflection of external reality; the book that finally decided me was Lenin's *Materialism and Empirio-Criticism*; this did say that emotion as well as the intellect reflected reality.'[7] With the detachment of hindsight, Upward sees the political commitment that resulted from this emotional response to an oppressive social reality as 'a kind of religious conversion'.[8] Stephen Spender, discussing Upward in 1935 on the basis of his two published short stories, observed that 'the most significant fact about Upward's two stories is that they are religious'. Spender saw this as legitimate and even desirable, suggesting a fairly widespread attitude towards political belief. He praised Upward as an example of the new kind of writer who would, by risking the 'destructive element' of contemporary reality, create a 'political or moral or sociological vision'.[9] In immersing himself in the destructive element however, the writer is wearing the armour of his belief, for this new religion protects the converted; in *Journey to the Border*, the hero's final commitment to revolutionary socialism is also an assertion of invulnerability: 'His decision to join the workers' movement would lead to difficulties. But he would at least have . . . begun to live. He had already begun. He had made a stand . . . *Nothing, no subsequent danger, could cancel that.*'[10]

George Orwell shared with Warner and Upward the equivocal attitude to Christianity. While he spoke out against the Catholic literary revival, he retained a benign regard for the remaining positive values of modern Protestantism. His dislike of 'popish' pomp and circumstance did not extend to the 'poor, unoffending old Church of England'.[11] His attitude was a combination of frustration with its irrelevance and affection for its Englishness and the way it seemed to symbolize the strength of ordinary existence. In 1932, Orwell was subscribing to the *Church Times*, and expressing his pleasure in seeing that there was 'life in the old dog yet – I mean in the poor old C. of E.'[12] His enthusiasm soon waned, however, when he felt the paper was descending to the level of 'the Romans' by becoming involved in theological squabbles.[13] He was not interested in a Church with ideas and dogma, but in a symbol, which with its conventional trappings of doddery vicars and charity bazaars would stand for the decency and integrity that he saw as threatened from every side. It was really a family affection; the Church of England was a slightly senile uncle to whom nobody paid much attention any more, but who nevertheless stood for something and would be missed.

The technological age seemed to be eroding the values for which the Church of England was a major repository, and Orwell feared that along with them would go the ability to create new ones; for technology was also changing the very basis of human behaviour. Orwell states the problem in *The Road to Wigan Pier*:

As for such qualities as loyalty, generosity, etc., in a world where nothing went wrong, they would be not only irrelevant but probably unimaginable. The truth is that many of the qualities we admire in human beings can only function in opposition to some kind of disaster, pain or difficulty; but the tendency of mechanical progress is to eliminate disaster, pain and difficulty.[14]

John Mander has called this 'a truly extraordinary statement for a man with a rationalist cast of mind',[15] but to call Orwell a rationalist, even by implication, is to beg the question. Orwell was only partly a rationalist. Another part of him, equally important, believed in a sort of fundamental life force, common to the mass of decent unpretentious people, which it was necessary to preserve. The continued existence of values such as tolerance, endurance, compassion and humility, depended for Orwell upon the individual's continued ability to recognize and to resist the evil of the world. The rational, mechanized, modern society threatened to reduce life to uniformity, the individual unable to recognize either evil or good.

Orwell's concern for social justice is a manifestation of his deeper, more intuitive concern for the survival of what he saw as the values essential to a civilization. The decision to assert the necessity of these values is also a decision to resist the encroachment of contemporary society upon the individual. Against this threat of uniformity, by which all actions would seem equally significant or equally meaningless, writers such as Greene and Waugh, Upward and Warner, posed a system of belief which defined action and asserted essential values. Orwell differed from his contemporaries in seeing Catholocism and Communism as working *against* such values – for him, these established beliefs were no more than tricks perpetrated by modern society luring unsuspecting believers into conformity and subservience. Nevertheless, he did share with his contemporaries the hope that somehow these underlying values could be convincingly defined and reasserted, before they disappeared altogether. In expressing the fear that with the elimination of 'disaster, pain and difficulty' would go the necessity for human forbearance and courage, Orwell was speaking for many of his contemporaries. Part of the attraction of revolutionary socialism was that it defined the evil in the world – capitalist oppression – and provided a place for just these kinds of virtues.

Warner's first novel, *The Wild Goose Chase*, published in 1937, exemplifies this notion. The hero, George, possesses the qualities of masculinity, modesty, and courage. In modern society these are no longer recognized as virtues, and he is regarded by his fellow-townsfolk as inferior to his bombastic and effeminate brothers; the society he inhabits is without any shared belief by which George may be judged for his true worth. In the quest which he undertakes for the wild goose, George seeks to re-establish, through social revolution, the connection between the people and the essential values of society; only a truly revolutionary society can convincingly define virtue. In *The Professor*, published in the following year, the liberal, rationalist hero of the title suffers because he assumes that a better society may be achieved by disregarding the 'living world', by ignoring those essential qualities of life that are beyond the reach of the unaided intellect. An old Christian acts in the novel as the spokesman for the inexplicable forces with which man must come to terms: 'Death and corruption are the strands out of which our life is formed. Lust and cruelty are tortures ingrained in the soul. How can we resist our world? Our world calls to us, not for resistance, but for love and for pity and for mercy.'[16] In common with Orwell, Warner regarded the existence of evil as necessary to the creation of positive values. The Professor's liberalism is mistaken, because it attempts to ignore altogether the inherent nature of evil. He recognizes that Christianity did once provide a framework by which evil could be recognized and satisfactorily dealt with, but the framework in modern times is offered by social revolution, which provides not only the means of coping with evil, but also the possibility of defeating it altogether. With clear symbolic intent, Warner presents the spokesman for

Christianity as an old man, whilst the voice of revolutionary action is his young son.

If romanticism may be defined as the desire for the synthesis of reality and ideal, then these thirties novelists were romantic in their aspirations. They turned away from rationalism and humanism, regarding the pragmatic and detached approach to the problems of the twentieth century as quite inadequate to the magnitude of the problems. They required an ideal that would both explain all of reality, and confirm its significance, and were generally unsympathetic to rationalist attempts to explain reality piecemeal. This dissatisfaction with pure rationality, with the virtues of scientific observation, is reflected in the strong streak of anti-intellectualism running through the thirties. Intellectualism itself was often equated with the tendency to deny the existence of spiritual or deeper values. Rex Warner is the most obviously anti-intellectual of the thirties novelists. He was opposed to the pursuit of disinterested knowledge, and preferred to see the spirit of inquiry as a function of revolutionary action. A large part of *The Wild Goose Chase* is devoted to indicating the ways in which dry intellectualism actually perverts the values of love and compassion. For Warner, scientific inquiry, conducted purely for its own sake, destroys the finer instincts. He allows an academic to damn himself in describing his own researches:

'Experiment . . . has enabled me . . . to draw up a calculus of sensation. I have experimented on animals and, if you will excuse me, on the bodies of unfortunate people, malefactors or votaries of science. On such occasions I have registered by various apparatus the rise or fall in the pressure of my own blood and in the blood of others who were spectators of these operations. . . . I shall never forget my agreeable perturbation when I first saw a woman roasted.'[17]

With blunt and righteous irony, the academic is authorially condemned for his failure to take account of deeper values. He lacks the morality by which he might judge his own work as perverted. Elsewhere in the novel, Warner uses the word 'intellectual' as an adjective of disapprobation, when he describes Professor Pothimere's 'thin intellectual lips and pointed chin'.[18] This attitude permeated the Auden group, and may be traced in part to Warner, by whom Day Lewis claims his own 'anti-intellectual bias had been set up'.[19]

The intellect was often seen by the writers of the thirties generation to function at the expense of the emotions and the instincts, those faculties which brought one closer to the essential forces in society. In *Coming Up for Air*, Orwell's hero George Bowling berates the scholar

Porteus for his absorption in intellectual pursuits, specifically because they cut him off from the important power of society: 'He's dead. He's a ghost. All people like that are dead.'[20] Not only is the pure life of the intellect sterile, it is also dangerous, for it facilitates the disintegration and dehumanization of society by ignoring the individual's need for a 'religious sense'. The conservative implications of anti-intellectualism are more obviously reconcilable with the political sentiments of Evelyn Waugh. He regarded any sort of rationalism, no matter how well intentioned, as folly, and his novels of the thirties combine to form a thorough-going rejection of humanism. In *Decline and Fall*, a prison governor is ridiculed for his modern schemes of prison improvement. As a direct result of his superficially rational policy, the prison chaplain is horribly murdered by a religious fanatic, an act motivated by human depths inaccessible to the rational mind. And, in *Black Mischief*, Waugh satirizes the efforts of the progressive Emperor Seth to popularize birth control by a poster campaign:

The poster portrayed two contrasted scenes. On one side a native hut of hideous squalor, overrun with children of every age, suffering from every physical incapacity – crippled, deformed, blind, spotted and insane; the father prematurely aged with paternity squatted by an empty cookpot; through the door could be seen his wife, withered and bowed with child-bearing, desperately hoeing at their inadequate crop. On the other side a bright parlour furnished with chairs and table; the mother, young and beautiful, sat at her ease eating a huge slice of raw meat; her husband smoked a long Arab hubble-bubble (still a caste mark of leisure throughout the land), while a single, healthy child sat between them reading a newspaper. Inset between the two pictures was a detailed drawing of some up-to-date contraceptive apparatus and the words in Sakuyu: WHICH HOME DO YOU CHOOSE?

Interest in the pictures was unbounded; all over the island woolly heads were nodding, black hands pointing, tongues clicking against filed teeth in unsyntactical dialects. Nowhere was there any doubt the meaning of the beautiful new pictures.

See: on right hand: there is rich man: smoke pipe like big chief: but his wife she no good: sit eating meat: and rich man no good: he only one son.

See: on left hand: poor man: not much eat: but his wife she very good, work hard in field: man he good too: eleven children: one very mad, very holy. And in the middle: Emperor's juju. Make you like that good man with eleven children.[21]

The natives do not suffer the brunt of the satire, for they have remained true to the spiritual values of their race. The Emperor's progress fails because it has been unthinkingly imposed, without any deferment to deeper values.

Both Warner and Waugh satirize the limitations of the rationalist mind, but it is, perhaps ironically, only Waugh who conveys a balancing sympathy for the victims of rationalism. Warner fails for the very reason so much left wing writing of the thirties does fail – the sheer obviousness, the bland inarguability of his sentiments. There are no shades of meaning, no seeds of doubt sown in the reader's mind. The moral point of the passage describing experiments on humans – that torture is evil – does not come as a revelation, but as a confirmation of respectable liberal values, values that even the most illiberal tyrant would at least profess to hold. The safeness of Warner's stand becomes clearer when contrasted with Swift's in *A Tale of a Tub*, which he seems deliberately to be echoing:

. . . in most corporeal beings, which have fallen under my cognizance, the outside hath been infinitely preferable to the in; whereof I have been farther convinced from some late experiments. Last week I saw a woman flayed, and you will hardly believe how much it altered her person for the worse. Yesterday I ordered the carcase of a beau to be stripped in my presence, when we were all amazed to find so many unsuspected faults under one suit of clothes.[22]

What is horrifying about the passage is the way in which scientific or aesthetic detachment, elements which the reader might well regard in other circumstances as virtues, are here applied to suffering and degradation. The reader is left to fill the gap between detachment and involvement and to pass judgement on the speaker. Warner's scientist however, is unequivocally condemned for the unscientific pleasure he takes in seeing a woman roasted. He is thereby dismissed as a monster, with whom the reader has nothing in common. Evil is characterized by Warner as evil, and good as good, and never the twain shall meet. Whereas Warner panders to the reader's complacency, Waugh, like Swift, uses our assumptions against us. We are implicated in the Emperor Seth's insensitivity and lack of vision because the language traps us. We smile perhaps at the over-zealousness of the poster campaign; but essentially we share the assumptions behind the campaign, assumptions which Waugh, reversing the interpretation according to the natives' point of view, elegantly sabotages.

Progress and rationalism both carry the threat of standardization, ushering in an efficient, mechanized world with little room for individuality. Waugh and Orwell and Greene focussed specifically on chromium plating, which seemed rapidly to be covering the world in a uniform sheen. The danger is that the individual will submit to standardization, imperceptibly sliding into acceptance. There is in many of the thirties heroes a determination to resist this process, a declaration of hatred for everything that is oppressive in the modern world. Orwell's Gordon Comstock for example, in *Keep the Aspidistra Flying* (1936), holds on to his individuality by maintaining a consistent pitch of anger; but anger in itself, without any possibility of relief, is presented as debilitating and unproductive. Comstock abandons his angry stand as much as anything from sheer exhaustion. Anger may, however, be seen as part of the progress towards belief, as in Edward Upward's short story 'Sunday' (1933), where anger is described as the first of the many stages of revolutionary action. Anger or hatred can lead to a recognition of the deeper forces at work in society, and hence to a renewed determination to resist oppressiveness.

The hero of the thirties novel must learn to survive in a threatening environment. He is almost always a version of Isherwood's 'Truly Weak Man', the sensitive, vacillating character who seeks strength through faith. In Greene's *Brighton Rock*, for example, the hero is able to survive the oppressiveness of Brighton gangland by relying upon the spiritual reserves of his Catholicism. The only significant communication in the novel is between the hero and his faith – by contrast, ordinary day-to-day living is described in *Brighton Rock* and in other thirties novels as baseless ritual. Words, supposedly the means by which ideas and feelings are conveyed, have become merely aids to social survival. They are important not for their semantic content but for their power to disguise emptiness. Repeated phrases or conversational mannerisms function as talismans. By their familiarity they give a much needed illusion of stability and continuity. In Orwell's *Coming Up for Air*, the hero's wife reacts to all crises, however minor, with the lament, 'I don't know what we're going to *do*.'[23] The very utterance affords some relief. It is a reflex action, like touching wood. In *Mr Norris Changes Trains*, Christopher Isherwood has his narrator recognize this aspect of the character of Mr Norris:

'Well, well,' observed Mr Norris, taking his cup, 'we live in stirring times; tea-stirring times.'

I grinned awkwardly. It was only later, when I knew him better, that I realized that these aged jokes (he had a whole repertoire of them) were not even intended to be laughed at. They belonged merely to certain occasions in the routine of his day. Not to have made one of them would have been like omitting to say grace.

Having thus performed his ritual, Mr Norris relapsed into silence.[24]

Mr Norris's little jokes are a modern parody of religious observance.

This kind of conversation, meaningful only to the speaker, but by which he gains a debased spiritual support, is one aspect of the thirties concern with social ritual. In *Keep the Aspidistra Flying* for instance, Gordon Comstock is obsessed with the rules of custom. He refuses to allow his *fiancée* to pay for him in a restaurant or on a bus because he sees it as an insult to his manhood. By failing to pay his own way he would be sacrificing his individuality. Ritual, although not based on any verifiable values or beliefs, remains the only means of self-definition. Similarly Anthony Last in Waugh's *A Handful of Dust* performs the weekly ritual of going to church. It is part of his duty as squire. Tony Last retains no religious faith, but paradoxically his regular attendance assumes great importance for him. The trappings of religion and the squirearchical tradition, although no longer based on universal certainties, still have the power to order an otherwise empty life. The ritual of church-going, like Mr Norris's conversation, has become its own justification, and is a measure of the hero's desperation.

Attempts by characters in these novels to assert and maintain their own significance are made in full consciousness of the threat of social chaos, and hence of individual insignificance. The individual who cannot comprehend or order his society will be unable to comprehend himself. Evelyn Waugh prefigures an absurdist universe in his expression of this fear of an incomprehensible world; cases of mistaken identity abound, and characters enter and depart from the plot without warning or explanation. Actions are arbitrary, motives unfathomable, and explanations misunderstood. Upward's tutor in *Journey to the Border* faces similar problems, misunderstood, or simply not listened to, by everyone with whom he comes into contact. Even when it appears that a group of people share common aims and ideals, it often emerges that they have their own private and unique reasons for doing so; thus the people who attend the party meeting in Greene's *It's a Battlefield* (1934), are ruthlessly broken up by Greene into a collection of individuals, amongst whom no meaningful communication is possible. Without genuinely common values, every individual is isolated, inventing his own rules.

Out of this sense of individual isolation, the thirties novelists give repeated expression to the desire for communication with someone who shares one's values and outlook at a profound level, and who therefore *understands*. In *Homage to Catalonia*, Orwell recalls such an instance of instinctive communication, with an Italian militiaman: 'it was as though his spirit and mine had momentarily succeeded in bridging the gulf of language and tradition and meeting in utter intimacy'.[25] This kind of spiritual intimacy is present between Crane and Chase in Greene's early novel, *Rumour at Nightfall* (1931), or between Eric and Maurice in Isherwood's *The Memorial* (1932) – as individuals they are incomplete, and only attain their full potential in the consciousness of their intimate relationship. The ideal of perfect communication, beneath the level of language and social ritual, is the subject of Isherwood's first published story, 'Two Brothers'. 'The understanding which existed between them was marvellous, it was a thing at which we only dimly guessed. They did not agree so much as fit perfectly together, like pieces of wood dovetailed.'[26] The twin, the brother, the *alter ego*, all offered instances of the kind of relationship the individual sought with the world, a relationship which would support his sense of self, paradoxically by merging him into something larger than himself. Such attempts to assert the status of the individual through instinctive relationships were shown inevitably to fail, or to be at best transitory. The 'utter intimacy' which exists between Orwell and the Italian militiaman lasts only 'momentarily'; Orwell also knows 'that to retain my first impression of him I must not see him again'.[27] The memory Orwell retains is emblematic of his desire to communicate utterly with his environment – it is not an end in itself. Thirties novelists did not regard personal relationships *in themselves* as a solution to the predicament of the individual, for meaningful relationships, even those based on this kind of instinctive communication, cannot continue to exist without common values and beliefs. Only when this instinctive understanding between two individuals is replaced by a shared means of understanding the world, a shared spiritual sense, can personal relationships be regarded as meaningful and permanent. The ideal, permanent relationship is not between individuals, but between believer and belief.

A great many writers discovered their spiritual sense in the idea of revolutionary action, and this is reflected in the large number of left-wing novels of the period. As the popularity of the Left Book Club demonstrated, there existed a large potential audience for any writing which adopted a left-wing or revolutionary standpoint. Journals such as *New Writing* and *Left Review* also catered to this audience, and in doing so actively encouraged the new, left-wing literature. They became to some extent victims of their own enthusiasm, in that the strong desire for a truly revolutionary literature, and particularly for a new fiction which would reflect the necessity for social action, led reviewers to make some exaggerated claims for particular works. There were, for example, a number of novels based on the events leading up to and including the Spanish Civil War, written generally from a pro-Nationalist and anti-clerical position. One of these, Ralph Bates' *The Olive Field* (1936), was declared by *Left Review* to be the 'finest revolutionary novel of our time',[28] and likened by as perceptive a critic as Edwin Muir to *War and Peace*.[29] These contemporary reviews of what seems today a very ordinary novel were by no means eccentric. Indeed they are typical of the kind of praise which greeted many novels of revolutionary or working class sympathies. The enthusiastic wish of reviewers for a serious and respectable revolutionary literature often led them to anticipate its achievement. Themselves committed or at least sympathetic to revolutionary socialism, they felt unable to condemn weaknesses of style or techinque, for in the battle of purpose against futility, and order against chaos, it was important to concentrate all the fire on the enemy.

The preachers of the new values felt it was up to them to help reverse the trend which English literature had taken in the preceding decades; the withdrawal of the artist into himself, the emphasis on feeling and personal emotion, the dominance of formal concerns, the importance of ambiguity and multiple suggestion. In *Viewpoint*, a magazine which appeared in 1934 and was rapidly incorporated into *Left Review*, an article called 'New Life for the Novel' summed up the situation as seen by the more intransigent of the left wing: 'Almost without exception the leading English novelists of today turn aside from the sight of starving humanity, standing in bread-queues, of harmless workers shot down in the streets, of all the evidences of a society drawing to its close, to plunge into the charting of their own individual souls. . . . The artist . . . must . . . participate in the revolutionary struggle, and above all, reflect that struggle in his work.'[30] The statement of the issues is rhetorical and unsophisticated, but conveys the frustration felt by those who pressed for the genuine revolutionary novel. In the same number of *Viewpoint*, the appearance and influence of a new vigorous poetry was regarded as a *fait accompli*: 'The cleavage between the so-called "Georgians" and the younger poets of today, is as wide as the difference between the typical eighteenth-century poets and *Lyrical Ballads*. . . . Youth is attacking in the names of Auden, Spender, Bottrall.'[31] In the first half of the decade at least, the novel was seen to be lagging behind poetry in the establishment of a vital political literature.

Left Review represented the more uncompromising left-wing criticism in the thirties, and was by no means full of unreserved praise for the middle-class poets of the Auden group. They seemed all too often to lack the quality of genuine anger that at least one left reviewer discovered in 'those blows at the self-satisfaction of contemporary society struck by Joyce, by the Dadaists, by the surrealists and the rest. . . . Hatred at least is a start.'[32] The journal resented often the schoolboy attitude of the middle-class poets to the serious matter of social revolution. Douglas Garman, reviewing a symposium entitled *Writing in Revolt* to which Stephen Spender had contributed, used the opportunity to attack the poet for the attitude he typified: 'He writes consciously as a Marxist and a Poet. . . . Unfortunately, however, since he may also be accepted as a Marxist, it is necessary to point out that the profundity of his theme is matched by the depth of his misunderstanding of Marx.'[33] But another reviewer gave the more pragmatic appraisal of the importance of Spender and his friends to the cause of social revolution. He regarded the good they were doing as far outweighing the harm. He observed 'a widespread interest directed, even though critically, towards the specific claims of Marxism. Part of the credit for this development belongs, (and must be given) to the three sometime Oxford poets, Auden, Day Lewis, and Spender – who, despite somewhat naive simplifications and inadequacies in their primitive geography, put communism on the poetic map.'[34]

Left-wing writers, whether committed or sympathetic to Marxism, tended to hold together in the face of a larger enemy. The writers who saw the social and political realities of the time as all-important in shaping their art were drawn together, despite internal dissensions which worked in the opposite direction and became increasingly obvious towards the end of the decade. While a generally left-wing literature was encouraged by a great many observers in the thirties, the kinds of distinctions possible *within* the term left-wing were neither very well understood nor rigorously explored. However, just as the middle-class poetry of the Auden group came up against a certain amount of resentment, so the middle-class left-wing novel often failed to satisfy unspecified revolutionary criteria. There is a vaguely defined awareness of two quite different kinds of left-wing novels, the proletarian and the middle-class. Closer examination reveals in fact three distinct sub-groups of left-orientated fiction. They are:

(a) The working class novel, often called by contemporary observers the proletarian novel, written from a working class or lower-middle class perspective.

(b) What may be called the 'socialist romance', written from a middle or upper-middle class perspective.

(c) The novel of specific socialist or revolutionary commitment, also written from a middle class stand-point.

The proletarian novel takes as its subject the everyday lives of the people who maintain an industrial society. One of the best and certainly the most popular of the novels in the sub-group is Walter Greenwood's *Love on the Dole*. It was a best-seller when it appeared in 1933, was successful as a play and a film, and has frequently been reprinted, an indication that it retains much of its power and interest. Part of its strength is in the evocation, by a man with first hand knowledge, of the sheer hopelessness of the lives of factory workers and their families. Greenwood does not, however, make any serious attempt to offer the means by which the sentiment of the epigraph might be implemented: 'The time is ripe, and rotten ripe, for change: Then let it come. . . .' Sally, the heroine, survives only by conscious cooperation with the degrading capitalist system, becoming the mistress of a wealthy bookmaker in order to provide for her family. The conclusion is neither affirmative nor negative, but a statement of the facts of life as Greenwood sees them. Extrapolating from the epigraph, it may be argued that the very existence of the novel constitutes a call to the barricades. But the movement within the book itself is towards frustration and cynical submission, not towards ideological commitment. The one politically active character in the novel, Larry, is a consumptive, who dies as a result of his efforts to organize an unsuccessful march against the Means Test. As Walter Allen says of another novel in this sub-group, Walter Brierly's *Means Test Man* (1935), 'one couldn't call it revolutionary or even in any sense political in its implications; it is essentially the cry of outrage of a serious-minded working man who has suddenly found himself deprived of function and status'.[35] The outrage is there but no solution or ideal survives the conclusion of the novel. Anger does not necessarily lead to commitment. L. G. Gibbon's trilogy, *A Scots Quair*, in many ways the most impressive of this sub-group, possesses in common with the work of Greenwood or of Brierly a sheer vitality that is often missing from the fiction of the middle class. Yet the conclusion of the novel is resigned and politically unambitious, marking a recognition by Gibbon of the split between the necessity for political action and the desire for personal gratification. Just as Greenwood's Larry gains nothing from his activism, so Gibbon's Ewan must renounce all personal feelings, attachments, and desires as a necessary requirement of political action. The end of *A Scots Quair* belongs to his mother, Chris, for whom political commitment is not a solution to the personal predicament. Her conclusion is also a kind of renunciation of expectations, an acceptance of the final irrelevance of individual action, and of the power of fate. 'She saw it now, sitting here quiet – that that Change who ruled the earth and the sky and the waters underneath the earth . . . might be stayed by none of the dreams of men.'[36] This recognition of a gap between social action and personal gratification signifies a vital difference between the proletarian and the left-wing middle-class novelists of the thirties. For the proletarian novelists, revolutionary commitment entailed the abandonment of all claims to individuality; for the middle-class novelists, revolutionary commitment and the desire for personal fulfilment were seen as interdependent, the one evolving inevitably out of the other.

The proletarian novel is political only in a rather special sense. It deals sympathetically with the oppressed class, and with the revolutionary urge, but it contains too the seeds of conservatism. The ultimate object is not to overthrow the capitalist system, but to come to terms with things as they are. Orwell commented on this aspect of the proletarian novel in speaking of Lionel Britton's *Hunger and Love* (1931). 'This was an outstanding book and I think in a way it is representative of proletarian literature. Well, what is it about? It is about a young proletarian who wishes he wasn't a proletarian.'[37] The last sentence is not frivolous; Orwell is simply reducing to its essence the common desire of the proletarian hero or heroine, to achieve a more favourable relationship with the *status quo* rather than fundamentally to change it. Writers such as Greenwood, Brierly, Gibbon and Britton were filling a need for literature about the working classes written by people with some idea of what it was like to be working class. Louis MacNeice describes the contemporary appeal of the proletarian novelist to the literary middle class, concentrating here on a group known as the Birmingham School:

At this time, 1936, literary London was just beginning to recognise something called the Birmingham School of novelists. Literary London, hungry for proletarian literature, assumed that the Birmingham novelists were proletarian. Birmingham denied this; take John Hampson, Walter Allen, Leslie Halward – Hampson was a friend of E. M. Forster and was not employed as a labourer, Allen was a graduate of Birmingham University, Halward was a plasterer's labourer but even he could not be counted as of the sacred proletariat – his father has been a small pork-butcher. It could be conceded however that they wrote about the People with a knowledge available to very few Londoners and that their view of the novel as social history had grown naturally out of their background instead of being, as in London, an apostasy from the view that the novel is primarily art.[38]

MacNeice is engaging in cultural nit-picking to question these writers' qualifications as true proletarians, but he does convey the

enthusiasm with which literary London greeted an authentically working class literature. This gratitude for authenticity was tempered by
disappointment that the novels did not go further. When Walter
Greenwood's second novel *His Worship the Mayor* appeared in 1934,
the *Left Review* praised its faithfulness to life only to conclude that it
'lacks ultimate direction, and its most serious fault is the complete
absence of any suggestion of a solution to the state of vulgar bigotry
and exploitation on the one hand and unrelieved misery and want on
the other.'[39] The proletarian novel, while it described conditions as
they were, failed to point to the necessity of political action, and for
this it was condemned.

The novels which did affirm this necessity sprang from the middle
class, and in particular from the influential writers associated with
Auden. Their influence in turn came not merely from their written
works, but from their public status as a coherent group with common, if not always clearly defined, aims. They shared a close similarity in age and background, an articulated reaction against Bloomsbury and the twenties, and a belief in the importance of the writer in
helping to effect the social revolution. Just as important were the
similarities of a more personal nature – a common belief in their own
talents, and an often exaggerated self-importance and seriousness.
All these factors combined to make a formidable group of young
writers who came to dominate the field of politically orientated
literature, and helped create a characteristic genre – the socialist
romance. This second sub-group of left-orientated novels often
typified what was most sentimental and unconsidered in the political
attitudes of the thirties. The social revolution was grafted onto a
conventional middle-class plot, often as a kind of *deus ex machina*,
releasing the hero from the limitations of his existence. The sub-
group contains the work of writers who often did not consider
themselves as novelists first, such as Spender, Day Lewis, and John
Lehmann, and of others who might possibly be termed serious
romantic novelists, such as Storm Jameson and Amabel Williams-
Ellis. The general character of these novels may be suggested by
looking briefly at one, John Lehmann's *Evil Was Abroad*, based
directly on his experiences in Vienna just before the *Anschluss*. The
main concerns of the novel are the hero's obsession with a young
Austrian working-class boy called Rudi, for whom he comes to feel
responsible, and the increasing awareness in the hero of political
conditions in Vienna and of the necessity of revolutionary action.
There is an attempt to show the interdependence of the personal and
the political planes, but too much is left unsaid for the attempt to

succeed. As is always the case with the socialist romance, the treatment of a complex subject remains superficial and naive.

The socialist romance was not necessarily greeted with enthusiasm by the literary left as a valid contribution to the cause. T. L. Hodgkin, in summing up Day Lewis' *Starting Point* (1937) for *Left Review*, outlined the weaknesses of the genre: 'his book makes grimly plain how much more difficult it is for the average English public-school and university educated novelist to apply the understanding of social processes to novel writing than it is to understand these processes. . . . The Communist Party is left an abstraction. All we know is that [the hero] joined the party because subjectively he found it more satisfying than stopping in his job as a schoolmaster'.[40] Hodgkin is unable to accept the arbitrary manner in which Communism is introduced into the novel. How, he asks elsewhere, can the middle-class novelist write 'a novel which will be at the same time revolutionary and the fruit of his own experience?'[41] And in an attack on the novels of Naomi Mitchison and Amabel Williams-Ellis (one of the original editors of *Left Review*), Q. D. Leavis raised a similar point, asking testily 'what confidence can be placed in the political "thought" of a writer who visualizes in terms of magazine-story situations, whose perceptions can be embodied in *pastiches* and *clichés*, and whose emotional equipment is no more refined than that of the bestseller of the corrupt bourgeois public . . . her [Amabel Williams-Ellis'] values are not personal, they are those of a "set", fashionable not intelligent'.[42] The aims of all the novelists of this sub-group, the conflation of the desire for personal fulfilment with the necessity of political action, were admirable, but the means of successfully doing so in the novel form eluded them.

There is however a third category, containing those few novelists who brought a measure of inventiveness to the task. Both Rex Warner and Edward Upward sought to establish convincingly through their fiction the validity of Marxism as the explanation and the exaltation of all reality; and as the cure for the individual malaise. Both writers were fringe members of the Auden group, and shared the common ties of background and education. They were prevented by this background from writing convincingly from a proletarian standpoint. The insipidity of the socialist romance was uncongenial, and the form itself unsuited to an effective statement of political commitment. Instead both Warner and Upward chose a combination of the picaresque and the fantastic, to describe a hero's progress towards political belief and political action.

NOTES

1. 'Fan-Fare' *Life* 20 (8.4.46) p. 56.
2. 'François Mauriac' (1945) *Collected Essays* (1969) pp. 115–16.
3. 'The Study of the Classics' *The Cult of Power* (1946) pp. 150–1.
4. *The Buried Day* (1960) pp. 219–20.
5. *Journey to the Border* (1938) p. 246.
6. Ibid.
7. 'A Conversation with Edward Upward' *The Review* 11–12 (1964) p. 67.
8. Ibid.
9. *The Destructive Element* (1935) pp. 242–3.
10. *Journey to the Border* pp. 255–6. Emphasis added.
11. 'Review' (1932) *Essays* 1 p. 81.
12. 'Letter to Eleanor Jacques' (19.10.32) *Essays* 1 p. 103.
13. 'Letter to Brenda Salkeld (extract)' (June? 1933) *Essays* 1 p. 121.
14. *The Road to Wigan Pier* (1937) p. 226.
15. *The Writer and Commitment* (1961) p. 88.
16. *The Professor* (1938) p. 255.
17. *The Wild Goose Chase* (1937) p. 180.
18. Ibid. p. 178.
19. *The Buried Day*, p. 219.
20. *Coming Up for Air* (1939) p. 196.
21. *Black Mischief* (1932) pp. 186–8.
22. 'A Tale of a Tub' *Gulliver's Travels and Other Writings* (1976) p. 333.
23. *Coming Up for Air* pp. 14–15.
24. *Mr Norris Changes Trains* (1935) p. 33.
25. *Homage to Catalonia* (1938) p. 2.
26. 'Two Brothers' *Oxford Outlook* 7 (May 1925) p. 110.
27. *Homage to Catalonia* p. 2.
28. Ralph Wright, 'New Novels' *Left Review* 2 (April 1936) p. 338.
29. 'New Novels' *Listener* 15 (29.4.36) p. 843.
30. D. E. Willis, 'New Life for the Novel' *Viewpoint* 1 (April–June 1934) p. 15.
31. Denis Botterill, 'Changing Gear' *Viewpoint* 1 (April–June 1934) p. 15.
32. 'Ajax', 'The Writer's War' *Left Review* 1 (November 1934) p. 15.
33. 'Writing in Revolt' *Left Review* 3 (September 1937) p. 498.
34. J. Brian Harvey, 'Proletarian or Pastoral?' *Left Review* 2 (February 1936) p. 231.
35. *Tradition and Dream* (1964) p. 229.
36. *Grey Granite*, p. 287.
37. 'The Proletarian Writer' (1940) *Essays* 2 p. 41.
38. *The Strings are False* (1965) pp. 154–5.
39. A. L. Lloyd, '*His Worship the Mayor* . . .' *Left Review* 1 (November 1934) p. 46.
40. 'The Individual and the Group' *Left Review* 3 (November 1937) pp. 628–9.
41. '*No Escape* . . .' *Left Review* 3 (March 1937) p. 109.
42. 'Lady Novelists and the Lower Orders' *Scrutiny* 4 (September 1935) p. 115.

Chapter 3

Novelists of Revolutionary Commitment: Edward Upward and Rex Warner

By the time *The Wild Goose Chase* was published late in 1937, and *Journey to the Border* early in 1938, the intellectuals' enthusiasm for revolutionary socialism had reached its peak and was even beginning to lose height. The political and literary allegiances of both writers had been made clear some years earlier by the inclusion of several poems by Warner, and two of Upward's short stories, in the famous *New Country* anthology of 1933. But neither author served an early apprenticeship in the novel form. While both belonged to the thirties generation – Upward was born in 1903, Warner in 1905 – their first novels appeared a decade later than those of their contemporaries, Waugh, Greene, and Isherwood, when they had all to a large extent left behind the emotional and intellectual uncertainties of the late twenties and early thirties. They were shortly to embark upon, and in some cases already experiencing the beginnings of the long process of reconsideration, modification, and sometimes rejection of the ideal and concerns of the decade. The short period between 1937 and 1938 formed a comparatively still point, marked by a temporary solidification of beliefs and self-confidence that may be seen in the publications of that time. In 1938, Graham Greene wrote his first explicitly Catholic novel, *Brighton Rock*, and Isherwood felt sufficient detachment from his immediate past and his formative years to produce the autobiographical *Lions and Shadows*. This atmosphere of comparative confidence and maturity is also behind the first novels of Upward and Warner. There are a number of important qualifications to be made about this kind of certainty – nevertheless, the dominant direction of both novels is towards a clear assertion of the necessity of revolutionary action. The complex mental processes by which one arrives at such an end, having rejected all other avenues, are stylized in both novels. The hero is guided through the maze of possibilities to the final affirmation. In this way, these novels stand as unusually clear statements of the movement towards belief characteristic of the generation – the initial dissatisfaction with society as it stands, the corresponding desire for the security and purpose of some kind of faith, the subsequent consideration of possibilities, and the final step, not always taken of course, of commitment to a single belief. Not only the first novels, but also the careers of Upward and Warner, correspond to this rough summary.

Within the Auden group, Edward Upward occupied a position of some authority. He was and has remained Christopher Isherwood's close friend and final critic. As schoolboys at Repton, they felt themselves to be united against 'them', a collective name for the other side, the system, seen through schoolboy eyes, that sought to destroy them.[1] The game grew more serious, particularly after Isherwood joined his friend at Cambridge: 'Our enemies, we liked to imagine, were perfectly well aware of our activities; they knew that we alone, of all the undergraduates in Cambridge, had seen through their tremendous and imposing bluff. Therefore, in due time, we should be dealt with.'[2] During one of their many walks together, an old door in a laneway suddenly became for them the doorway into The Other Town, an escape from Cambridge and the pressures of reality into a half-whimsical, half-menacing private domain. The accidental phrase 'The Rats' Hostel' provided the 'keywords which expressed the innermost nature of the town', becoming, Isherwood recalls, 'gradually defined in our minds as a name for a certain atmosphere, a genre: the special brand of medieval surrealism which we had made our own. (I use the term "surrealism" simply for the purpose of explanation: we had, of course, no idea that a surrealist movement already existed on the Continent. . . .)'.[3] This exclusive, mysterious world assumed increasingly literary proportions and was eventually given its name. It is not perhaps too much to see expressed in the conflation 'Mortmere' their reaction against the oppressive and inadequate values of the past, the consciousness of being different from the established society embodied in the mother. After they had left university, Mortmere, now characterized as a village on the downs, populated by murderous eccentrics, remained alive as a private creation, becoming less and less private as it was described to other, newer friends.[4] This retention and dissemination of Mortmere, which continued amongst the Auden group well into the thirties, was not simply a one-way process, indicative of the adult desire to recapture the cosy security of schooldays. The schoolboy unity of us against them, Isherwood and Upward's fancy that two undergraduates alone could see 'through their tremendous and imposing bluff', prefigures Upward's movement towards Marxism, his deliberate allegiance to the 'us' of the proletariat against the 'them' of capitalism. Something of the Mortmere atmosphere survives and colours the adult commitment, helping to preserve the quality of youthful righteousness that characterizes the literary Marxism of the thirties.

This remains true even though by 1930 Upward had quite deliberately rejected Mortmere and its quality of Gothic irrelevance that
Isherwood associated, not altogether helpfully, with surrealism. The
only direct result of this early imaginative partnership was Upward's
short story 'The Railway Accident', written in 1928. The attempted
evocation of an 'other' world, unfamiliar and yet recognizable, is
adolescent and forced:

Up the bleached gravel-drive, oppressed by ink-dark trees. Lilac bifurcated
past the windscreen in perfumes of wan blue gauze. Odours of chimes of
croquet hoops, tango of views of choirboys throught the rustling privet. A
lawnmower wove its rainbow fountain along imagined rock and fern. . . .
The front door was held open by the brass head of a fox. Summer mildly
billowed into a hall shadowy as a cave. . . .[5]

The language strives to create an atmosphere, but the writer seems
more at home with the familiar than the unusual; the passage, for
example, in which the hero's train companion, a headmaster, describes a teacher's indiscretions in the dormitory, points beyond the
superficially anarchic Mortmere world to its roots in the schooldays
of Upward and Isherwood. The Mortmere atmosphere does however
possess at its best a disconcerting intensity that is used to effect in
Journey to the Border, where the exaggerated or heightened novel-
reality coexists more happily with the formal, almost allegorical
structure of the novel. After 1928, the dislocated world view
presented in 'The Railway Accident' began to be harnessed to political didacticism. By 1929, in the story 'The Colleagues', social revolution has already become the focal point of the creative act. The
recognition by a young schoolmaster of the forces of reaction in all
their horror is expressed as a kind of mystical experience or revelation. Subsequent stories, 'Sunday' and 'The Island', follow a similar
pattern but move further towards the corollary of such a revelation,
positive social action. They begin by inveighing against the present,
using something of the grotesqueness of the Mortmere world to
catalogue the properties of an ordinary but malignant universe; 'the
table, the flower with protruding stamens arching from its jug like a
sabre-toothed tiger, the glass of custard, pleated apple-green satin
behind the fretwork fleur-de-lis pattern of the piano'.[6] The violence,
the sexual aggression, the evil all implicit in this description, force a
reaction, commitment to change through social action. Commitment
defines action, or in this case, immediate action; the first few steps are
clear: 'He will go out into the street and walk down to the harbour. He
will go to the small club behind the Geisha Cafe. He will ask whether

there is a meeting tonight. At first he may be regarded with suspicion, even taken for a police spy. And quite naturally. He will have to prove himself, to prove that he isn't a mere neurotic, an untrustworthy freak. It will take time. But it is the only hope. He will at least have made a start.'[7] Upward's language is here very close to Isherwood's description of their school and university days – the recognition of the Enemy, and the consequent binding together of these few who see clearly the conspiracy against them. In the small club behind the Geisha cafe begins an Audensque journey to another country, and only the chosen will survive the trip. Upward's hero will need to 'prove himself', for commitment to revolutionary socialism is also a test of individual worth.

Upward's three early stories are comparatively little known today, in spite of being reprinted in Penguin Modern Classics, but this last passage, from 'Sunday', is often quoted. Julian Symons sees it as a particularly striking example of the 'curious . . . disparity' which existed in left-wing, middle-class writing of the thirties, 'between the tone of absolute certainty in which these revolutionary sentiments were uttered, and the actual situation'.[8] Samuel Hynes quotes the same passage, but remarks that 'it is a sign of the political uncertainty of the time that this nervous last home – set, one notes, in the future tense, as a possibility only – should be taken as an example of political decisiveness, or for that matter as political writing at all'.[9] Despite their differing assumptions about the tone of the passage, both writers effectively chastise Upward for his ignorance of political realities, and his failure to offer rather more specific means by which the revolution may be encouraged. Hynes points quite rightly to the vagueness of Upward's conclusion, which may in turn be interpreted as tentativeness; there is, in addition, something disturbingly blinkered and unsympathetic in the references to 'mere neurotic' and 'untrustworthy freak'. But Upward is not offering nor claiming to offer a blueprint for social action, and it is not altogether fair to dismiss him for failing to do so. The emphasis in 'Sunday', or indeed in Upward and Warner's fiction generally, is upon the *act* of commitment, and this must be given its due weight. The act of commitment was seen by both novelists as its own continuing justification. From Upward's 'The Colleagues' to Warner's *The Professor*, the *consequences* of belief in revolutionary action, and the details of implementation, are never contemplated except in the most general terms. The new world remains in the undescribed future – the decision to act for a new society, against the obvious trend of European events, was regarded as a sufficiently assertive and positive act in itself. Indeed the word 'commitment' can only be used, in connection with the thirties generation, in a predominantly verbal sense. The decisions both to believe, and to take the first step necessary to conform to the rules of the belief, are the focal points of these novels of revolutionary action, and here lies the satisfaction for the believer.

In the late twenties and early thirties, Upward was an object of awed respect for a small group of writers. Lehmann describes in his autobiography how he had 'heard with the tremor of excitement that an entomologist feels at the news of an unknown butterfly sighted in the depths of a forest, that behind Auden and Spender and Isherwood stood the even more legendary figure of an unknown writer, Edward Upward'.[10] As a Communist and a party member, he encouraged the existing interest of his fellow writers in political events, and helped to direct it. Stephen Spender for example recalls that as a result of a conversation with Upward in Berlin in 1932, his outrage and despair over the political situation in Europe began to move 'along lines laid down by Marxist arguments'.[11] Christopher Isherwood had always regarded Upward 'as his literary mentor', and by 1930 'it seemed that he might become Christopher's political mentor, too'.[12] But Isherwood sees a fundamental difference in their political attitudes; for his own part, he lacked seriousness. He began to regard Upward as a conventionally pious Catholic might regard a friend who had made up his mind to become a priest.[13] The choice of comparison is by itself suggestive, but it reveals as well the particular quality of the admiration felt by Isherwood and the other writers of the Auden group for Upward as a genuinely committed revolutionary.

Upward maintained the responsibility of the writer to reflect Marxism as the most satisfactory means of 'explaining spiritual realities (i.e. thoughts and feelings) in terms of material realities (i.e. nature and human society)'.[14] Literature must be true to the superficial, oppressive reality of contemporary society, while at the same time pointing to and reasserting deep spiritual values. Upward, in his 'Sketch for a Marxist Interpretation of Literature', is resolute about the kind of literature required, rather more vague however on how to go about it. For that one must look to *Journey to the Border*, in which he seeks to provide an artistic corollary to the assertion that the only valid method of defining the individual existence is belief in the inevitability of revolution. Upward seeks to create too a novel world which is only given positive direction by the introduction of social action as a defining force.

Rex Warner shared with Upward the belief that the novel could fulfil an educative function, by providing the catalyst which pointed to the necessity of political action. 'We have learnt that a novel can exercise as much (or even more) political influence as can a procession or an official leaflet. So long as men have the leisure and the desire to read, literature is sure to be a force not only in life but in politics.'[15] Warner's attitude to social revolution was however more equivocal than Upward's. While Upward regarded the recognition of historical necessity as a revelatory experience, marking a surgical break from the fumbling bourgeois past, Warner was more prone to see Marxism as the legitimate heir of nineteenth century liberalism, embodying the sort of general humanitarian notions to which any right-thinking man or woman would subscribe; 'nowadays, as has often been pointed out, one need not be a Marxist, one need only be an ordinary decent person, to approve the immediate practical aims of Marxism'.[16] There is a disarming naivety in this appeal to middle-class notions of decency and common-sense as a justification of Marxism. By concentrating on its 'immediate practical aims', Warner paradoxically reveals his lack of concern for the *detailed* aims of Marxism, emphasizing instead that the act of commitment or even of approval will *of itself* help to change the nature of society. Warner felt the values for which Marxism stood to be unarguable, but these values as he expressed them could be unhelpfully vague. In the title essay of the collection published at the end of the Second World War, *The Cult of Power*, Warner criticizes D. H. Lawrence for his attempts to build a system based on 'blood and sex', and concludes that 'the only reply to the cult of individual or racial power and violence is the actual practice of general justice, mercy, brotherhood and understanding'.[17] More overtly than most, he regarded Marxism as a sort of pagan saviour who gave to these values of justice and mercy an inviolable status. This saviour is symbolized by the wild goose, which must be pursued if happiness and personal fulfilment are to be achieved. Cecil Day Lewis recalls Warner as an undergraduate swinging 'more and more wildly between ideal and real',[18] and Warner himself became increasingly aware of the dependence of one upon the other. In literary terms, he maintained that 'pure observation undirected by imagination or moral impulse' was 'almost meaningless',[19] that the mere presentation of reality could not of itself provide a sense of life's significance and purpose. Warner's 'moral impulse' is provided in *The Wild Goose Chase* by belief in social action, which in turn links the individual with the mysterious, immutable values in his society. In the story of one man's faithful pursuit of the 'wild goose', there is a clear link with the tradition of quest literature. The mood of youthful enthusiasm which attaches to the hero's quest does however gain further definition when compared with an earlier work, *The Kite*, which Warner contributed in 1936 to a series of adventure stories for boys. *The Wild Goose Chase* is also a kind of adventure story, in which the goody sets out to defeat the baddies.

It is the quest that recurs throughout the thirties. The hero undertakes a journey to another, faraway place, looking for confirmation of his own significance. Such journeys may be seen not only in Auden's early poetry, but in the travels of Basil Seal to Africa or Tony Last to Brazil, of Greene's Anthony Farrant to South East Asia or Isherwood's heroes to Berlin. It can be seen in the absurd peregrinations of Blore-Smith in Anthony Powell's *Agents and Patients* (1936), and its negative correlation in the frustrated journey of Henry Green's characters in *Party Going* (1939). What these novels have in common is the movement away from a specifically English world, without any consequent loss of the essential Englishness of the hero. The hero sees, in certain aspects of middle-class English society, threats to his individuality and his desire for fulfilment or simply for fun. Whether it be in the blameless but dauntingly conventional background of Blore-Smith, or in the almost expressionist novel-world of Warner or Upward, the author's concept of a repressive society remains recognizably English and recognizably middle class. At the same time the hero retains the virtues of his upbringing, which might be summed up as a core of decency, or to be unkind, of unimaginativeness, that prevents him succumbing to the foreign country.

The nameless hero of Upward's *Journey to the Border* is a version of the sensitive young man from public school and ancient university who crops up in much of the fiction of the twenties and thirties. Upward's tutor shares with these modern heroes the fear and directionlessness that is one result of uncertain times. He is closely related to the Truly Weak Man, whom Isherwood describes by comparison with a 'truly strong man'. The latter, 'calm, balanced, aware of his strength, sits drinking quietly in the bar; it is not necessary for him to try and prove to himself that he is not afraid, by joining the Foreign Legion, seeking out the most dangerous wild animals in the remotest tropical jungles, leaving his comfortable home in a snowstorm to climb the impossible glacier. In other words, the Test exists only for the Truly Weak Man.'[20] To adopt for a moment Isherwood's highly self-conscious symbolism, the thirties hero is unable to ignore the snowstorm outside; as a truly weak man, his imagination and sensitivity force upon him an awareness of the oppressive or confusing nature of reality, at the same time revealing to him a choice: to accept, with resignation or despair, the impossibility of coping, or to confront the conditions of existence and by some means triumph over them. Such a definition applies to Upward's tutor, to Tony Last, Pinkie Brown or Gordon Comstock, to the narrator in Powell's *What's Become of Waring* (1939) or to Naylor in Cyril Connolly's *The Rock Pool* (1936). For each of these heroes, and for others like them, the conventional social world he inhabits and understands and relies upon, grows increasingly bizarre and perhaps threatening. Even those heroes who begin, like the 'truly strong man', with an implicit assumption of control over their lives, grow more disorientated and confused, and begin to seek some solution to their predicament.

The tutor in *Journey to the Border* progresses from fear and indecision to direct political commitment. The progress is described as a movement from disease to health, from the threat of insanity to true sanity. Despite setbacks, the tutor never retreats into the refuge of complete despair, but remains poised, with varying degrees of precariousness, 'on the border' – between madness and sanity, sterility and fulfilment, political confusion and political action. Throughout his vicissitudes, he is consistently aware of what he requires, a requirement that does not significantly diverge from its initial statement on the second page of the novel:

. . . it would be . . . some act which would violently break the continuity of his life as a hired tutor. It might be a bogus ceremony of purification, performed in the kitchen or in the stable loft or under the dining-room table or on the croquet lawn. He would symbolically wash off all the dismal servilities of the past three months. . . . It would be something more than a frantic and temporary reaction against three months of self-effacement. Yes, it would be the beginning of a new technique, a first step towards solving the problem of how to live. . . .[21]

He remains aware that the preservation of his sanity, of his integrity as an individual, depends upon the clear perception of the real world and his function within it, and that this will only be achieved under the aegis of some ordering system or belief he is yet to discover.

This initial statement of intent contains Upward's notion of the ritualistic element in any future commitment – the active decision to accept the inevitability of social revolution at the end of the novel is presented too as a 'ceremony of purification'. At the beginning the tutor can only envisage this ceremony as 'bogus', but the genuineness of revolutionary socialism renders the act of commitment genuine too. Whereas the acts the tutor imagines earlier in the novel are purely symbolic, action becomes, under Marxism, both symbolic and practical. At the end of 'Sunday', for example, when the hero seeks out the back room of the Geisha Cafe, his physical act of commitment is securely presented as an important contribution to the cause. At the same time, it is a ritualistic or ceremonious act. The novelistic conventions of spy story and thriller to which the final paragraph of the story alludes help to invest an apparently mundane act – walking into a café – with significance. Just as a clandestine meeting in a sordid back room will prefigure a chain of consequences in a spy or detective story, so the similar description at the end of 'Sunday' holds the weight and significance of all action to follow. The act of commitment, or perhaps more accurately the decision to perform this act in the immediate future, marks in 'Sunday' and in *Journey to the Border* a dramatic change in the significance of personal action. Revolutionary socialism provides the ordering system within which action is rendered significant. If insanity may be acceptably defined as the inability to cope with or order reality, then Upward's parallel between sanity and political commitment becomes quite clear. The individual who fails to accept the validity of revolution is in Upward's terms 'insane', because he is without the means of coping with the real world. In a conversation with his *alter ego*, the tutor arrives at an understanding of the meaning of his insanity, and of the necessity of political action. ' "Let us suppose," says his other self, "that you actually have been insane: you can be sure that, if your disease is curable, you could not find a better way of curing it than by joining the workers' movement. Because there is no other way of dealing *successfully* with the real external problems which confront you." '[22] Yet the final commitment seems as much an arbitrary cutting-off as a clear conclusion. Revolutionary socialism does not emerge with any compelling logic as the true 'cure' for the hero's condition, though the act of commitment itself is immensely significant. Upward conveys the sheer necessity of belief. The weight of conviction that revolutionary socialism does assume at the end of the novel springs not from logical justification of its appropriateness to the hero's, and by implication the reader's predicament, but from this act of commitment. In other words, the very fact that Upward's hero decides irrevocably upon a course of revolutionary action helps to endow revolutionary action with the power and irrefutability that he requires from a belief. The relationship between hero and belief is thus a reflexive one, each awarding the other a necessary significance.

The relationship between hero and belief in Upward's novel indicates the vital difference between Marxism *per se* and what may be termed for the sake of brevity 'thirties Marxism'. According to D. E. S. Maxwell, 'it was the purely intellectual structure of Marxism that engaged Edward Upward',[23] but the evidence for his claim is slight. It is certainly true that Upward was more concerned with the details of Marxism than were his contemporaries in the Auden group, but this intellectual interest was a function of a deeper emotional commitment. In an interview in 1964 Upward was asked 'just how personal were the pressures that brought [him] to Communism'. He replied: 'I was much more deeply immersed in the theoretical side of the politics than the other imaginative writers I knew. At the beginning of *In the Thirties* the hero comes to Communism as a kind of religious conversion, and this represents my own attitude. I came to it not so much through consciousness of the political and economic situation as through despair.'[24] The suggestion of an intellectually rigorous approach to Marxism in the first sentence is quite flattened by what follows. The short stories, *Journey to the Border*, and Upward's own recollections, all indicate that however absorbed he may have become in the theory of Marxism, the dominating impulse was an instinctive reaction against the times, the essentially romantic search for the consolation of belief.

The major problem facing Upward and Warner was the appropriate choice of novel form to express the relationship, as they understood it, of individual to society. The apparent choice was one between realism and imagination, between the naturalistic presentation of society typified by the proletarian novel, and the creation of a novel-world whose features would refer only obliquely to the real world. Because Upward and Warner favoured the latter course, their decision might seem to have been a clear one. There was, however, another implied choice, one that corresponds but is by no means the same as the opposition of realism and imagination – the choice between tradition and experiment. It is by now a commonplace that the left-orientated writers of the thirties were drawn to the traditional, established modes in literature and particularly in the novel, and not as the term 'revolutionary' could suggest, to the experimental. To make it new was seen by many as directionless and irresponsible, not a questioning of the basis of society but a retreat into word-games. Warner and Upward subscribed to this notion, but felt at the same time impossibly bound by it. The aim of their novels was the presentation not just of society but of the individual consciousness, a task which seemed to call for rather more than accumulated detail if it was to present convincingly the hero's state of mind. Upward has recalled the dilemma: 'I naturally wanted to experiment: I felt very strongly that it was necessary for socialist art to find new forms, not merely a new content. I was dissatisfied with the idea that you could take over the Balzac novel and just decant a new content into it. But I must confess that in my weaker moments I did feel that there was something slightly disreputable about experiment. I still feel that, say, *Finnegans Wake* was a dead end, and that one couldn't go on from that.'[25] Experiment was 'disreputable' because of the attitude towards it of the literary left-wing, as exemplified by *Left Review*, and there is in *Journey to the Border* a noticeable conflict between Upward's concern to present imaginatively the progress of the individual towards belief, and his desire to conform to rather simple notions of social and political relevance.

This conflict can be seen more clearly in Warner's *The Wild Goose Chase*. In order to preach the desirability of commitment to social action, Warner rejected the ambiguity of formal manipulation in favour of straightforwardness and honesty. At the same time he was with Upward distrustful of undiluted realism or 'reportage' – the proletarian novel indicated that such a method sacrificed moral and political didacticism. The result is a mixture of methods and forms – mythic quest novel with popular adventure story, the clarity and common-sense of a revived seventeenth-century prose co-existing with interior monologue. The importance Warner places on clarity of style is based upon his belief that 'the greatest allegorists, such as Swift and Bunyan, have been at the same time the greatest masters of prose style',[26] because 'great care is necessary in order to win the reader's confidence in the illusion which is being put before him'. The novelist must write with 'precision of detail and assurance in the reality of what is invented'.[27] Reality and imagination are thus united. George, the hero of *The Wild Goose Chase* states his own literary preferences as 'Shakespeare . . . Karl Marx, Tom Jones and Isaiah',[28] in defiance of the superficial modernism favoured by the academy in which he finds himself. As far as these writers can be grouped under any one heading, they seem to embody for the hero and for Warner the proper balance of creative imagination and relevance to the real world. Warner is similarly careful in the construction of his own imagined novel-world to create at the same time a structure of contemporary references, so that for example various of the villains in *The Wild Goose Chase* can be reconstructed as contemporary political figures. This precision of correlation confirms the link that Warner implies between himself and Swift or Bunyan, in that their works also function simultaneously on the imaginative and the realistic level, and the full potential is realized only through an awareness of the relationship between the two levels. These links with English writers of the past seem now more illuminating than the supposed influence upon Warner and Upward, made much of at the time, of the writings of Franz Kafka. In Upward's novel, there is a similarity of mood arising from the nature of the subject – a man searching for a way out of a terrifying maze. And Warner's novels actually seem to contain specific echoes of Kafka; there are, Kafka-like, endless corridors, enigmatic seductresses, bland inquisitors, as well as the structural similarity impossible to verify as imitation – the repeatedly frustrated quest for the centre of meaning. Such links, however, obscure the vital differences. Unlike Kafka, Upward and Warner write with an object in mind, revolutionary action. And the worlds they create, whatever their superficial resemblances to Kafka, are thoroughly English ones.

Indeed *The Wild Goose Chase* can be seen as a modern pilgrim's progress, with George as everyman who embarks upon his quest and will not be deflected from his goal. At the same time George is not simply everyman, but a particular hero whose individuality Warner is at pains to establish. In order to do so, he deviates in two important respects from his distanced allegorical method. In Part Two the detached narration is temporarily abandoned and the first person assumed through the device 'he said to himself'.[29] And Warner makes an attempt to convey the immediacy of George's individual reactions earlier in the novel by resorting to a highly derivative stream-of-consciousness technique: 'Mouth broke to smile and eyes spilt sparkles (Oh, lovely, thought George, that warm mouth, the burstingness of) as she stood still holding the handle of a basket, holding back, knowing the life coiled within, braced and barred by cloth (Oh, long lovely the straight limbs, George thought, must be, with shapely catenation of breast curves and the flank and sweeping of buttocks.)'[30] Such ham-fisted appropriations of the experimental mode, with their echoes of Hopkins and of novelists of the preceding generation such as Joyce and Woolf, are not uncommon in the fiction of the thirties, and quite out of line with the common feeling of reaction against them.

In 1935, Orwell published *A Clergyman's Daughter*, with its distinctly unsuccessful 'night town' chapter, and in the same year the stream-of-consciousness cropped up in Graham Greene's *England Made Me* and in his curiosity in limited edition, *The Bear Fell Free*.

Christopher Isherwood's first novels were written very much in the shadow of Bloomsbury, making free use of the interior monologue. None of these attempts are genuinely experimental, but imitative of an earlier generation. None of these novelists did more than dabble in the possibilities of such formal manipulation. Yet the reasons for the passing interest were valid ones. Their concern was primarily with the predicament of the individual, and while they differed from their predecessors in seeing this predicament as bound up with the contemporary world, they shared their elders' concern to penetrate and describe the mind of the hero. Stream-of-consciousness and interior monologue form a small part of their attempts to do so. But for Warner, and for Orwell, Greene, and Isherwood as well, the primary object was to convey, in Warner's phrase, an 'assurance in the reality of what is invented'. For these younger novelists, stream-of-consciousness, whatever its attractions, stood for something quite different, a highly personal, imagined world whose connection with their understanding of reality was by no means clear.

The variations upon the detached parabolic structure of *The Wild Goose Chase* are illuminating, but they are variations only. The parable dominates, reinforced by the mythic quality of the quest itself, the departure of three brothers, Rudolph, David and George, into the unknown in search of the wild goose. Rudolph and David are deflected from their goal, but George continues the quest. He meets Joe, who crossed the border many years ago and joined in the revolution against the tyranny of the City, which ended in the defeat of the rebels. George's experience in many ways echoes Joe's, suggesting the continuous nature of the revolutionary journey; George moves further towards the achievement of the social revolution than Joe, but his is not by this fact the archetypal successful quest. His pursuit of the wild goose is one of many such journeys which have been undertaken in the past and will doubtless need to be undertaken in the future, one of an accretion of personal political quests that form the fabric of continuous social action. All those who like Joe and George remain single-minded in their pursuit of the wild goose contribute to the eventual permanent defeat of the forces of oppression.

If the wild goose is accepted then as the object of the quest, one must at some stage come to terms with the idiomatic implications of the title. At the beginning of the novel, Warner establishes the veracity of his narrator by describing briefly an incident from the future, in which an old man, half-mad, returns from across the border claiming to be the wreck of the young George. The narrator reconstructs the consequent story from information received from this mysterious figure. This suggestion of George's ultimate fate is not referred to again, but the implications of defeat are reinforced by the concluding sentence of the novel. George has already led a successful revolution, eliminating both oppressors and deviationists within the revolutionary party, though the King has escaped to fight another day: 'Be the future as it might be, and no doubt that complete success was distant still, he knew that something not unworthy had been achieved already as he stood with the men and women, holding Joan's hand in his hand, and observed some of the Generals looking at him with an odd expression in their eyes, and their mouths smiling.'[31] Clearly battles lie ahead, and George's search for the wild goose is by no means over. The quest is a 'wild goose chase' in the sense that it may never end and the wild goose will always be elusive. And yet how conscious was Warner of the further implication – that the wild goose does not exist, that the chase is a mere diversion? The title itself points to a persistent sub-stratum of doubt that pervades this super-ficially confident novel. Like Upward, Warner does not contemplate any final object of revolutionary action. He envisages instead contin-uous and unending action, a permanent revolution. The undoubted energy that *Journey to the Border* and *The Wild Goose Chase* possess springs in large measure from the tension between the individual and his society, between rebelliousness and oppression. The endings of both novels are not simple resolutions of this tension – they are instead assertions that this same tension will continue into the indefi-nite future; so that the final emphasis of both novels is upon the necessity of continuous action, continuous commitment. Yet this is in itself a kind of escape from consequences. On the surface both novels take troubled but determined paths to revolutionary action. But beneath the surface lies the central, unresolved conflict, between the desire for individuality, and the desire to belong. What looks like a confrontation with important issues is in the end another form of escape.

Escapism and the attraction to Communism went hand in hand in the thirties. Julian Symons quotes from Auden's 'Psychology and Art' on the subject of escapism in art:

'There must always be two kinds of art, escape-art, for man needs escape as he needs food and deep sleep, and parable-art, that art which will teach man to unlearn hatred and learn love.' This remark was used as a justification of much that Auden perhaps did not intend, but it is certainly true in the sense that the dream of the Thirties comprehended both earnestness and irresponsibility. . . . It may be true that in the end the attempt to blend parable-art and escape-art is a sort of schizophrenia, doing severe mental damage. The desire to do so, and the belief that it could be done, was an integral part of the Thirties dream. . . .[32]

In Symons's interpretation of Auden's terms, both novels are clearly parable-art, each following a similar basic pattern in order to point a political moral. At the same time, each novel is to some extent 'escapist', though that term itself is difficult to define. They are escapist in that commitment to revolutionary action offers a way out; the nature of that way out, and the consequences of taking it, are barely described. They are escapist too in that Upward and Warner seem in their novels to return to the unrealistic simplicity of the schoolboy world, where the out-of bounds areas are strictly defined, and the presentation of genuine social action is backed by a notion of schoolboy heroics. This second definition equates escapism with simplicity, which is in its turn characteristic of parable-art. In other words, the term 'parable' itself contains at least one notion of escapism, the desire to simplify and stylize and *uncomplicate* reality. In these terms, *Journey to the Border* and *The Wild Goose Chase* are escapist *by virtue* of being parabolic, and the two are not, as Symons suggests, incompatible. The parable however, if it is to achieve its aim of pointing a moral, cannot be *simply* escapist. Parable simplifies in order to clarify, but the novel world must also be capable of being reconstituted by the reader in real terms – the relevance of the parable must be apparent. One thus returns by a circuitous route to one of the basic problems that confronted Warner and Upward as political novelists – the problem of social relevance.

It is important here to draw a distinction between the novels as they stand, and Upward's and Warner's presumed intentions. The intentional fallacy notwithstanding, it may be assumed, from the associations of Warner and Upward in the thirties, from their occasional writings, and from evidence within the novels themselves, that *Journey to the Border* and *The Wild Goose Chase* were written with didactic intent. But to judge on this basis is to declare them failures; despite the dominating presence in both novels of social or revolutionary action, neither novel points conclusively to its necessity, nor convincingly to the means of implementing it. Yet to demand this of any novel is in effect to demand the impossible, to impose criteria by which no work should be judged. The novels are politically ineffectual in the sense that they will not necessarily make revolutionaries out of readers, but they *are* relevant to the human desire for significance, and it is in these terms that the 'parable' must be reconstructed.

They are statements of the desire for what may be called in thirties terminology a 'new country', the assertion of the individual's power and need to pursue an ideal. In *The Wild Goose Chase*, the ideal is embodied in the geese themselves, and at the end of the novel their cry is heard once again by George. They are a reminder that the individual must continuously challenge his society, and be continually on guard against complacency. In the title itself there is the implication that the ideal may not even exist, but this does not invalidate the quest, for the constant resolve to maintain the quest is itself guarantee of the individual integrity. The element of tentativeness or uncertainty that attaches to the conclusions of both novels serves only to emphasize the importance of commitment as an act of faith. Whatever may be the intellectual justifications of political belief, there is a gap of uncertainty between individual and belief that can only be bridged by the sheer will to believe.

In these novels the hero stands out against a background of chaos and confusion, and such affirmation as the novels possess depends greatly upon the hero's resolve to maintain this relationship with his environment. Belief in revolutionary socialism provides the strength and direction to the hero's self-assertion, but his self-assertion implies an essential corollary, namely an oppressive society. Yet in the ideal society to be achieved by revolution, society and individual will be compatible, and self-assertion a meaningless concept. In effect, the hero's confidence in his own significance *depends* upon a repressive society in the face of which he may assert his individuality, aided by his commitment to revolution. Warner and Upward do not proceed to a logical conclusion, the presentation of the achieved revolutionary society, for this would involve in a fundamental way the negation of the hero.

From this it seems that an entirely positive revolutionary novel is an impossibility, unless, rather like Malraux's *L'Espoir*, it eschews the individual hero in favour of some notion of revolutionary society as hero. Otherwise the touchstone of the novel becomes the actions and concerns of a single man rather than of society as a whole. Warner recognizes, without resolving, the dilemma caused by the desire to assert the power of the individual,. and by the implication of Marxism that the individual is in fact subservient to deeper social and historical movements. When George lectures on Othello to the students of the Convent, he refers to Shakespeare's 'unlimited admiration for those who, however mistakenly, follow a grand idea and are fanatical, ingenuous, pig-headed'.[33] This kind of admiration is behind Warner's attitude to George, admiration for the individual who believes in something, even if it is only himself, and asserts his heroic stature by sticking rigidly to that belief. Yet despite his 'grand idea' and his innate nobility, Othello is no match for the corruption around him; George claims that 'in spite of his apparently pusillanimous behaviour, Othello was after all a heroic figure, a figure of great and noble simplicity terribly ruined by contact with a completely false system of values'.[34] The only protection against a 'false system of values' is faith in the eventual triumph of a true system, the future society based on Marxist principles. Othello's beliefs are false, and consequently his innate nobility cannot save him.

The suggestion is that only belief in social action can prevent the submission of even the most 'heroic' figure to the corrupt society. Heroic action is *by itself* unproductive; as George says to himself: 'How clearly do I see now that the city and its kind can never be subdued, never even be seriously disturbed by adventurers! Only an army, only the organized movement of masses can shake that Government, and my place is on no pedestal of my own, but shoulder to shoulder with the peasants and with what portion of the town populace may be ready for revolt.'[35] The contradiction here is at the core of Warner's thirties fiction: heroic action, either for its own sake or as part of a mistaken belief, is self-indulgent and self-defeating. It will change nothing and the corrupt society will triumph. True self-fulfilment and individual purpose can only be achieved through social action, but this also involves an abnegation of conventional notions of the hero and heroic action. George realizes that he cannot be a conventional hero for his achievements are thereby unreal – the kings he fights are story-book kings, with no relation to social reality. He must deliberately join forces with all other individuals who seek to destroy the present society, forfeiting his uniqueness and thereby his heroic stature. Taking this process to its logical conclusion creates unresolved doubts about the individual's continued existence *as an individual*. Commitment to political action brings with it individual purpose and importance, while paradoxically denying the importance of the individual.

This paradox is never really resolved in *The Wild Goose Chase*, which helps to explain the final uncertainty over the fate of George. Does he retain his position as individual and hero at the end, or does he, as the opening pages of the novel suggest, merge into the revolutionary struggle, sacrificing himself for the cause? There is in the prefatory chapter, which deals with George's ultimate fate, the suggestion of a resolution (a suggestion that is taken up in Warner's subsequent novel, *The Professor*). George is described as returning to his hometown physically shattered and mentally unbalanced, but with something to impart: 'Go into the marshes yourself. Reclaim the land. That is where you will find George.'[36] George's personal quest has clearly failed, but at the same time he is accorded a symbolic heroic status. As one who has tried and failed, he embodies the desire for, and belief in, a new society. If they ignore him and treat him as simply mad, the townspeople will be rejecting the call to action and denying the significance of George's experience. If they accept the call to 'drain the marshes', they will be affirming anew the desire for revolution. They will be reclaiming George, assuring that his own quest has not been in vain, asserting in retrospect the significance of his actions. George would be defeated finally, but would also survive, like Joe before him, as an heroic example. None of these qualifications of the status of the hero in *The Wild Goose Chase* can however obscure the fact that the novel is centrally concerned with George, and, by implication, with maintaining his heroic stature. He does not finally merge into a larger context, because his individuality has been too carefully established and maintained. By sheer amount of space that is devoted to him, if nothing else, he must remain an individual and a hero. Revolutionary socialism is important in these novels because it *supports* the hero in his desire to maintain his individuality and his quest. It is the means by which he continues significantly to exist, rather than a cause to which he is consciously subservient. Warner is aware that the novel advocating revolutionary commitment demands a radical reconsideration of the function of the fictional hero. But such a reconsideration is beyond his powers, or indeed his desires. *The Wild Goose Chase* is a novel of revolution, but it is by no means a revolutionary novel.

Neither Warner nor Upward are in the front rank of modern novelists, and there is little to be gained, least of all for the reputation of political literature in Britain, by pretending otherwise. They are, however, in the context of their time, interesting and even admirable for what they attempted. Their novels illuminate both the problems that were faced by their literary class, and the problems that were not. They grabbed onto Marxism with a kind of desperate complacency, convinced of its application to them, yet failing ever to ask any really serious questions about what such a belief meant for the future. There is a profound uncertainty in Warner's and Upward's work, an uncertainty that pervaded the middle-class literary left and rendered it, or so it seems in retrospect, so ineffectual. The heroes of both novels are young and middle class, and their primary concern is, not unusually, themselves. The possibility that conscious commitment to revolution might demand another set of attitudes entirely is never really confronted. Neither hero develops in any way; instead, it is almost as if they stand still, watching the action pass by, accepting an illusion of progress. For, like their contemporaries in the Auden group, Warner and Upward took only the most perfunctory steps towards Marxism. Instead they made Marxism, or a version of it, come to them. *The Wild Goose Chase* and *Journey to the Border* are in the end conventional rather than original works not least because revolutionary action, the pivotal point of both novels, is used to confirm rather than question a thoroughly bourgeois hero.

The problem of the individual's relationship to society seemed for Edward Upward an insurmountable one, so much so that he did not publish fiction again for twenty-four years. Belief in revolutionary socialism, which on the one hand seemed to support individuality, seemed also, quite contradictorily, to be threatening it. He felt, in other words, that his belief in Marxism might convincingly order his fictional universe, and place his hero within it, but at the same time he felt the consequent restrictions upon his own freedom as an artist: 'It is very easy to deceive oneself about creative processes,' he later recalled, 'but I see it like this: I came to regard literature as serving politics . . . I believed in those days that a poem should be a political statement and not, as I believe now, a poetic statement – what stopped me writing was, I suppose an artistic conscience. I was trying to produce a political statement and not an artistic statement.'[37] Warner was also concerned to arrive at a less contradictory relationship of writer and belief, hero and society. On the one hand revolutionary socialism offered the means by which the writer could proceed to a fruitful conclusion, and the means by which the hero could maintain his individuality. On the other, it imposed restrictions upon the creative process, and it implied the eventual disappearance of the hero, in favour of the new society he was helping to bring about. Warner's subsequent novels of the period, *The Professor* and *The Aerodrome*, return to the problem, and may be seen as variations upon a solution.

In *The Professor*, published in 1938, the hero of the title is not a young man with a cause, but a middle-aged intellectual whose life has been based on civilized liberalism. His values are supported not by a belief with rules or dogma, but by confidence in what is right and what is wrong, of what is decent and what is uncivilized. For Warner, such confidence was misplaced, because it failed to recognize the *ad hoc* nature of such a system of values, and its consequent vulnerability. In his attitude to the Professor's humanism, Warner echoes the sentiments of his generation, the ambivalent attitude towards those of their elders who could not simply be dismissed as corrupt or criminally irresponsible. For every arms-manufacturer or sadistic house-master there might be someone like the Professor, who was of the wrong generation and ignorant of the real forces at work in society, but whose personal and artistic priorities could be admired. Christopher Isherwood exemplifies this mixed reaction in his recollection of Virginia Woolf: '(Despite Christopher's admiration for *Jacob's Room*, *Mrs Dalloway* and *To the Lighthouse* . . . he sometimes used Virginia as an enemy-image of the ivory-tower intellectual. For instance, after he and Stephen had been to see *Kameradschaft*, Pabst's film about the coalminers, in 1931, Christopher told Stephen that, when the tunnel caved in and the miners were trapped, he had thought: "That makes Virginia Woolf look pretty silly").'[38] Similarly, the Professor's calm reasonableness may be sympathetic, but it is also dangerous, a luxury that can only be safely indulged when the revolutionary society has been established.

The Professor is a cautionary tale. The hero embodies all those qualities that will flower unthreatened in a truly socialist society, but he must give way to the struggle to achieve that society. The civilized values and pleasures, the concern with self and with personal relationships, must all be suppressed in the struggle against fascism. The argument is a familiar one in the revolutionary rhetoric of the thirties, and is particularly associated with the years 1937 and 1938, when it seemed that such a battle was actually being fought in the Spanish Civil War:

> Tomorrow for the young poets exploding like bombs,
> The walks by the lake, the weeks of perfect communion;
> >   Tomorrow the bicycle races
> Through the suburbs on summer evenings. But to-day the struggle.

> To-day the deliberate increase in the chances of death,
> The conscious acceptance of guilt in the necessary murder;
> >   To-day the expending of powers
> On the flat ephemeral pamphlet and the boring meeting.[39]

Auden's lines effectively sum up the difference between those who, like the Professor, rely on the power of civilized values to survive unaided, and those who, like his son, demand the necessary sacrifice in order that these values might be re-established in a revolutionary society. The Professor's communist son, aware that the values of his father are inadequate, speaks not for the worth of the individual, but for the necessity of belief, of submission to the 'dictatorship of an idea'.[40] Unusually among his contemporaries, Warner here faces the essential paradox of 'thirties Marxism', the underlying conflict between the assertion of individuality, and the commitment to a future revolutionary society in which individuality is explicitly sacrificed to the cause. When the Professor is shot, Warner in effect kills off the only individualized character in the novel, his place taken by his son who is by contrast a mere representation of necessity.

In *The Professor*, revolutionary action assumes an importance it does not possess in either *The Wild Goose Chase* or *Journey to the Border*. It acts no longer as a support for the individual, but as a controlling agent, suppressing all claims to individuality. In this respect Warner followed through his beliefs of the thirties in a way that Upward did not. At the same time he was unable to abandon altogether the concept of individuality, for it is described as undergoing a temporary eclipse only, to be reasserted in the future, when the revolution has been achieved. A clear distinction is thus made between the period of revolutionary action, and the resulting new society. In Warner's terms, the achieved society, which remains outside the scope of the novel, will provide a secure and permanent system of values upon which individuality may flourish. Only in the struggle to achieve that society can the concern with self be seen as irresponsible, for there can be no meaningful or permanent understanding of self without a permanently and commonly-held system of values. *The Professor* can therefore be seen as the result of Warner's reconsideration of the relationship between individual and belief. In *The Wild Goose Chase*, George's significance as an individual depends finally on the continued existence of a corrupt society, and thus the continued necessity for revolutionary action. *The Professor* however maintains that true individuality and independence of mind, such as that claimed by the Professor himself, can only exist in a society based upon profound socialist principles, where these principles are accepted unconsciously by everyone as the source of common values. The present demands conscious commitment to these values, and hence a conscious renunciation of one's rights as an individual, in order that those rights be established as inviolate in the future.

'The future' is contemplated in different terms in *The Professor* than in *The Wild Goose Chase*, but in neither is it described. In his third novel, *The Aerodrome*, published in 1941, Warner considered much more directly the implications of his own need for belief and 'a purpose in life'.[41] The personal importance to the author of the issues involved in *The Aerodrome* is emphasized by the first person narration and by the similarity of the hero-narrator's name, Roy, to his own.

Roy is caught between two worlds, the traditional and increasingly irrelevant values of a kind of idealized rural England, and the dynamic future embodied in the aerodrome. As the first stage in an intricate plot based on uncertain parentage, Roy discovers himself to be an 'orphan', and not as he had supposed for his twenty-one years, the son of the village rector. Warner's own background, as 'a son of the rectory',[42] suggests a strong autobiographical element, but Roy's isolation from the values of his upbringing, and the urgent need to establish a new function and significance for himself, speak not just for Warner but for the predicament of his generation. When the rector declares Roy's true parentage to be unknown, Roy's response is 'Who am I then?',[43] signalling in the first chapter of the novel Warner's return with full attention to the central motivation of his thirties fiction, the individual's search for significance through belief.

The paradoxical nature of Warner's political beliefs emerges in Roy's attitude to the village of his childhood. The society in which he has been brought up appears to him as both comforting and corrupt, attractive yet purposeless. Pubs and football and church-going are the emblems of a civilization that has become rotten, but the emblems themselves retain a certain intrinsic value that Roy is not prepared wholly to deny. The Air Vice-Marshal offers the solution to his dissatisfaction and rootlessness in a career as an airman, a figure who retains in Roy's eyes – if not the author's – all the dramatic strength and purpose he possesses in Auden's early poetry. He is the true hero, one of the few to reject the past and embark upon the dangerous quest, the 'helmeted airman' for whom 'the clouds rift suddenly'.[44] This romantic notion of heroic action is also behind *The Wild Goose Chase*, but in *The Aerodrome* Warner confronts its fascist implications. The aerodrome offers discipline and a cult of purposeful action, but as Roy discovers, its real purpose remains disturbingly vague. Sex, emotions, finer feelings are all subordinated to the cause. The cause itself is self-generating and self-justifying. In *The Professor* Warner advocates the temporary suppression of individuality, but *The Aerodrome* questions whether it is too great a sacrifice to make. The aerodrome is a self-contained society which thrives on the standardization of its citizens – it is not a stage of the revolution, but an end in itself. The new society is as oppressive as the old, and it inevitably creates its own rebels. The conclusion of *The Aerodrome* is a kind of elegy, a sad rejection not only of the 'old order' but of the 'new order' as well.

The desire for belief, particularly with reference to the thirties generation, may be seen as the desire to comprehend, to define the world and hence one's position in it. The conclusion of *The Aerodrome*, which is also the conclusion of a three-novel exploration of the relationship of individual and belief, is an acceptance of the incomprehensibility of the universe, a final acceptance of limitations. Published in 1941, the novel reveals already a detachment from the thirties experience, a desire to explain and evaluate it. It marks in its way the end of a particular road, and it seems logical therefore that Warner should afterwards turn away from political fiction and pursue instead a career as a classicist and historical novelist. Upward on the other hand did return in later years to the issues raised in his thirties work, with the publication in 1962 of his novel *In the Thirties*. The gap of twenty-four years inevitably accentuates its retrospective, analytical quality. It may best be termed an autobiographical novel, part of a trilogy now complete, that is the most explicit, if not the most immediate account of the young middle-class writer's predicament in the late twenties and early thirties. The hero, Alan Sebrill, is on holiday at 'the bay' at the invitation of his friend Richard, a character based upon Christopher Isherwood. Alan feels he is doomed to a meaningless existence in a hostile society. Poetry and life are equally without purpose. 'This was a state in which he could not bear to continue, no matter what action he might have to force himself to take in order to escape from it.' During a solitary walk, he considers the courses open to him:

> He wanted to go on living, but not in the same way as now. 'What can be done to make life bearable?' he thought, as he began walking along the path that ran parallel with the cliff-edge. There was no hope in poetry, nor in love.
>
> He would turn for help to religion. . . . Other poets, far better poets than himself, had turned to Rome. The main difficulty would be the first step of getting himself to believe in the premises on which the Catholic religion was based: after that – so he had read somewhere – he would find that all the rest of it followed on quite logically and reasonably. Yes, but would he ever be able to believe in the premisses. . . .
>
> How much more easily he could have accepted Marxism . . . if he had not already found that it was of no help to him as a poet. But why hadn't it helped him? Perhaps because he hadn't even begun to be a Marxist yet. 'Philosophers hitherto have merely interpreted the world,' Marx had said: 'the thing is to change it.' To be a Marxist Alan would have to take action in the external world, which meant that he would have to become a Communist. Then there might be hope for him. Communism was the only force in the world which was uncompromisingly on the side of the doomed and against those who wanted to keep them doomed. . . . He must join the Party for its own sake, make it his supreme interest, set all his hopes on it.[45]

In contrast with his attitude in the thirties, Upward here comes to terms with the over-riding importance of the desire for belief, and the subsidiary importance of the belief itself. Religion, and particularly Catholicism, is considered as a possible means of personal salvation from despair, but is rejected ostensibly because of the impossibility of ever believing in its 'premisses'. Yet in the final statement of intention Upward suggests not so much the inherent credibility of the premisses of Communism, but his hero's determination to believe in them at all costs. Belief comes not as an inevitability but through an act of will. The essential difference between Catholicism and Communism is the failure of Catholicism to place any great significance upon 'action in the external world'. For Upward and for his hero, belief must offer temporal change; it must in other words do more than simply *explain* reality, it must show the way to *change* it permanently. For Upward then, Catholicism is essentially a passive belief, one that must be simply accepted as the explanation of all reality. Communism on the other hand involves the believer in meaningful action, so that the function of individual existence is a tangible one. The progression of Upward's hero is from despair, to the attraction of religion, to belief in social action. For Upward's contemporary, Graham Greene, the elements were the same but the order different – from despair, to the attractions of revolution, to religious conversion.

NOTES

1. See *Lions and Shadows*, particularly Chapter Two.
2. Ibid p. 67.
3. Ibid p. 70.
4. *World Within World* p. 102.
5. *The Railway Accident and Other Stories* (1969) p. 35.
6. 'Sunday' (1933) *The Railway Accident* . . . p. 53.
7. Ibid p. 58.
8. *The Thirties* p. 32.
9. *The Auden Generation* (1976) p. 107.
10. *The Whispering Gallery* p. 195.
11. *World Within World* p. 133.
12. *Christopher and His Kind* p. 42.
13. Ibid p. 43.
14. 'Sketch for a Marxist Interpretation of Literature' *The Mind in Chains* ed Day Lewis (1937) p. 45.
15. 'On Freedom of Expression' *The Cult of Power* p. 126.
16. 'Education' *The Mind in Chains* p. 36.
17. 'The Cult of Power' *The Cult of Power* p. 20.
18. *The Buried Day* p. 161.
19. 'The Allegorical Method' p. 107.
20. *Lions and Shadows* p. 207.
21. *Journey to the Border* p. 9.
22. Ibid p. 215.
23. *Poets of the Thirties* (1969) p. 88.
24. 'A Conversation with Edward Upward' p. 67.

25. Ibid p. 66.
26. 'The Allegorical Method' p. 112.
27. Ibid p. 116.
28. *The Wild Goose Chase* p. 174.
29. Ibid p. 231.
30. Ibid p. 90.
31. Ibid p. 442.
32. *The Thirties* pp. 68–70.
33. *The Wild Goose Chase* p. 186.
34. Ibid p. 185.
35. Ibid p. 233.
36. Ibid p. 35.
37. 'A Conversation with Edward Upward' p. 66.
38. *Christopher and His Kind* p. 90.
39. *Spain* (1937) p. 11.
40. *The Professor* p. 88.
41. *The Aerodrome* (1941) p. 138.
42. *The Buried Day* p. 161.
43. *The Aerodrome* p. 26.
44. Auden, 'Consider' (1930) *Collected Shorter Poems* (1966) p. 49.
45. *In the Thirties* (1962) pp. 39–42.

Chapter 4

The Catholic Novelist I:
Graham Greene

Graham Greene's conversion to Catholicism took place in 1926, but it was not until 1938 that he published the novel, *Brighton Rock*, that asserted the validity and the necessity of religious belief. In 1970, Greene offered his own explanation for the delay:

> More than ten years had passed since I was received into the Church. At that time, as I have written elsewhere, I had not been emotionally moved, but only intellectually convinced. . . .
>
> My professional life and my religion were contained in quite separate compartments, and I had no ambition to bring them together. It was 'clumsy life again at her stupid work' which did that; on one side, the socialist persecution of religion in Mexico and on the other General Franco's attack on Republican Spain inextricably involved religion in contemporary life.
>
> I think it was under these two influences – and the backward and forward sway of my sympathies – that I began to examine more closely the effect of faith on action.[1]

By his own account, Greene's religious commitment was a private and considered act, very much removed from questions of the relationship of Catholicism to a specifically contemporary world. Instead Catholicism provided an intellectually satisfying but at the same time rather abstract explanation of the world and the meaning of existence, one whose very logicality compelled belief. In making this kind of distinction Greene is denying any personal need for belief; he is claiming that the predicament of the young man seeking permanence in a dangerously impermanent society was not his predicament – instead Catholicism presented itself to him as possessing the irresistible logic of mathematics. There is however an inherent paradox in Greene's description of himself in 1936 as 'a Catholic with an intellectual if not an emotional belief in Catholic dogma',[2] and in his reiteration of this sentiment half a life-time later.

Greene's distinction between intellectual and emotional belief is vital to an understanding of the relationship of the novelist to belief in the thirties. Edward Upward uses virtually the same terms to discuss retrospectively the basis of his political commitment, and in doing so concedes to an emotional or personal motivation towards belief that he tended very much to deny in the thirties. Evelyn Waugh on the other hand, writing in 1949, employs the same distinction in order to establish, with Greene, the dominantly intellectual motivation of his conversion. 'It only remained to examine the historic and philosophic grounds for supposing the Christian revelation to be genuine. I was fortunate enough to be introduced to a brilliant and holy priest who undertook to prove this to me, and so on firm intellectual conviction but with little emotion I was admitted into the Church.'[3] This distinction is an artificial one in the sense that purely emotional or purely intellectual belief are impossibilities, but at the same time the implications of both terms are clear. Intellectual belief denies or substantially reduces the importance of the individual's background and personality and circumstances in the decision to believe. It is a logical, and by implication unimpeachable process, by which any rational human being might become convinced of the validity of Catholicism or indeed of Marxism. Emotional belief, by contrast, emphasizes the personal need for faith, the willingness to accept belief without a rigorous understanding of premises or dogma. It carries implications of weakness or immaturity. Both Greene and Waugh, in their insistence upon the intellectual basis of their belief, reveal an awareness of these secondary implications, and their possible imputation to themselves. Yet to adopt this distinction as a critical yardstick, and to judge Greene and Waugh's fiction of the period in terms of its success in justifying intellectual commitment to Catholicism, is a fruitless exercise; as fruitless as it is to judge the fiction of Warner and Upward by its ability logically to justify belief in Marxism. Belief, when it appears in these novels, is important not as an independent phenomenon, but as an aspect of the hero's predicament. It is, in other words, predominantly personal or 'emotional' belief that informs the novels of the period – the relationship of belief and individual believer, and the effect each has upon the other.

Both Greene and Waugh claim to have been convinced by the indisputable validity of Catholic dogma, and to have accordingly had no option but to become converts. The emotional or instinctive belief emerged only gradually, complementing and perhaps finally overwhelming the intellect. In his autobiography, Greene quotes approvingly an old priest who has been questioned on the reasons for his faith: 'I knew them once, but I have forgotten them.'[4] Once the intellectual groundwork has been laid securely, it is safe to cover it with the luxury of emotional belief. By this initial and single-minded concern with the rational validity of Catholicism, Greene and Waugh were taking out insurance upon their faith. Emotional belief carries with it the strong possibility of later disillusionment, if and when the

tenets of the faith seem increasingly to diverge from reality. But if it i
first established that the faith covers convincingly all aspects of re
ality, the possibility of disillusionment is eliminated. Greene's de
scription of his faith as intellectually compelled is in effect a claim fo
the irrefutability of religion. But there is a final disingenuousness t
the claim: it is possible intellectually to understand the means b
which Catholic doctrine explains and justifies the individual exist
ence, but the understanding will not *of itself* lead to conversion. Th
initial impetus must spring from a need for, or at the very least
predisposition towards faith. Greene's state of mind as a child an
adolescent, described in his autobiography, strongly suggests such
need. His retained memories – of a man in a workhouse cutting hi
throat, of a dead dog in a pram, of a tin jerry full of blood – seen
contrived, but they convey the morbid sensitivity of a child lost in
confusing and threatening world. Greene's recollections present the
most powerful image of the rootlessness and uncertainty that char
acterized his generation. His pessimistic world view required
powerful belief to prevent progress towards complete nihilism.

The emotional basis of belief, the instinctive pull away from despai
towards the security and self-justification of faith, is glossed over b
Greene in his autobiography and other reminiscences, but it may b
seen at work in his fiction of the thirties, particularly in the two earl
novels that have since remained out of print at the author's instiga
tion, *The Name of Action* and *Rumour at Nightfall*. Greene has expresse
his puzzlement at the failure of public and reviewers to recognize hi
Catholicism until 1938; 'I had become a Catholic in 1926, and all m
books, except for one lamentable volume of verse at Oxford, ha
been written as a Catholic, but no one had noticed the faith to which
belonged before the publication of *Brighton Rock*.'[5] Indeed an earlie
novel, *It's a Battlefield*, was seen by *Viewpoint* (later *Left Review*) ir
1934 as a welcome example of the kind of fiction they advocated. 'A
yet English novelists show few signs of advancement in this direction
[i.e. of depicting the revolutionary struggle] though Graham Greene
in *It's a Battlefield* has some conception of the basis of the class
struggle which he depicts against a wide and varied social back
ground.'[6] While it is true that Greene was not regarded as a Catholi
novelist until 1938, he has himself been partly responsible for en
couraging the idea that *Brighton Rock* was his first 'Catholic' work. Ir
an interview in 1957 he claimed that for a decade after his conversior
he 'simply hadn't had sufficient experience of how Catholics think o
behave, and therefore . . . couldn't write about them'.[7] The force
of the word 'couldn't' is ambiguous. As a piece of self-criticism it ma

well be valid, yet Greene seems also to be suggesting that he *didn't* write about Catholics, that his incomplete understanding of Catholic motivation and sensibility actually prevented him tackling the subject. But, as he puts it, 'by [1937] the time was ripe for me to use Catholic characters'.[8] In both these comments there is a muddiness of intention that seems to confirm rather than deny the notion that Greene only began to be a 'Catholic novelist' with *Brighton Rock*. In fact, Catholicism and Catholic characters are by no means absent from the earlier novels, and in *The Name of Action* and *Rumour at Nightfall* they play a considerable part.

The hero of *The Name of Action* is a wealthy and bored young man named Oliver Chant, whose need to break out of his purposeless existence leads him to the Palatinate with the vague aim of financing a revolution. The confusion between Chant's personal and political motives increases as he becomes infatuated with Anne-Marie Demassener, the wife of the Dictator. Against a background of violence, intrigue and self-aggrandizement, Catholicism is posed as a secure source of permanent values for those fortunate enough to have inherited their belief. When Chant questions his lieutenant, Weber, on the loyalty of some supporters, he receives the reply: 'They are all good Catholics' – as though he held some standard that had nothing to do with elementary schools or priests or even attendance at Mass.'[9] The 'as though' is not ironical; it reflects the puzzlement of the outsider when faced with such an irrefutable 'standard'. Catholicism for Weber is above the mundane and the everyday, offering an enviable security. Weber's wife is the embodiment of Catholic solidity: 'She spoke with a certainty which could never have been troubled by needs, questionings, doubts, analysis. That, thought Chant with some bitterness, was a haven to which neither he nor Anne-Marie Demassener could ever come. They were born in an age of doubt and to a class which wished to know too much.'[10] Chant's heritage is a modern one, a dry rationalism which offers him little comfort. He and his generation have lost contact, apparently irrevocably, with the spiritual certainty possessed by Frau Weber. In an attempt to still and satisfy the 'needs, questionings, doubts, analysis', he places his hopes first in political action, then in sexual love. Both fail him, and the recognition of failure comes to him in a church, 'where God was not a cloudy aspiration but a concrete hope or fear. . . . He had believed in freedom. . . . He had believed in love. . . . It had seemed to Chant that he had been enabled to see the boundaries of the infinite. "O God, O God", he murmured . . . "I wish that I could believe in your infinity."'[11] Twentieth-century scepticism which has moulded Chant's personality now prevents commitment to the mysterious faith which would resolve his spiritual crisis and offer him the certainty he requires. It is the emotions that are drawing him towards commitment, and the intellect, the curses of doubt and analysis, that hold him back. He belongs to a generation of explainers, but the power of Catholicism is presented as quite inexplicable.

Rumour at Nightfall, published in the following year, is set in Spain during the Carlist Wars. Crane, an Englishman and a man of reason, is attracted to a darkly romantic, aristocratic Spanish woman who possesses the certainty of faith: '"It seems to me that you must know everything which is worth knowing." His eyes swept back across the room, up the wall to the crucifix. He stared at it with a sceptical hope of enlightenment. "I envy you." He had seen the effect of belief on many people. He knew it was regarded as a recipe for peace, an ingredient of courage.'[12] Catholicism in these two novels is always described in such portentous and mysterious terms, and fits fairly well within the format of the romantic adventure story. Greene takes a modern, rational, directionless man and places him in the context of another faith, another tradition. The hero reacts with envy and a crudely articulated desire for the certainty of belief, but he does not, or rather cannot, make any meaningful connection with the ancient faith. Its promise of fulfilment remains tantalizingly unattainable to the rationalist mind, because any connection that is made is on an emotional level only – the intellect remains stubbornly unresponsive. Catholicism in these two novels belongs to the past, not to the sterile modern age, and like the past it is irrecoverable. Both novels can be seen as statements of the problem facing the twentieth century man attracted to religious commitment; they point both to the emotional need for faith, and to the impossibility of overcoming scepticism. At the same time there is an element of bitterness and contempt in these descriptions of Catholics and Catholicism, a suggestion that Frau Weber's 'certainty' might also be smug and simple-minded. Frau Weber's religion completely pre-empts needs and questionings and doubts, but Catholicism must be capable of answering needs, and resolving doubts, if it is to appear at all meaningful to a Chant or a Crane. The gulf separating the modern Englishman from the consolation of faith is emphasized by Greene's placement of his self-questioning heroes in conventional adventure-story settings – the romanticized nineteenth-century Spain of *Rumour at Nightfall*, and the equally romanticized Palatine Republic of the twenties in *The Name of Action*. The opposition of scepticism and Catholicism thus corresponds to the opposition of realism and romance, of relevance and irrelevance. Catholicism maintains a shaky presence in the novels by its association with the mysterious and romanticized settings, but by virtue of this association, it also seems to have no connection with the predicament of the modern hero. As Greene began to abandon what may be termed serious romantic fiction, and to concentrate more closely on the reality of the thirties, it became increasingly difficult to maintain even this balance. In a novel with a modern, realistic, and hence for Greene almost exclusively depressing setting, there would seem to be little room for asserting the presence, much less the validity, of Catholicism.

From *Stamboul Train* (1932) onwards, Greene's novels of the thirties clearly reflect a world without values. This notion of a foundering, purposeless society, heading inexorably towards chaos, is characteristic of the times. Its corollary was the desire for security and order through some kind of belief, and Greene was as aware as anyone of the claims of Marxism to fill that role. He has always inclined to the left in his political views, and indeed while an undergraduate at Oxford had been for a brief time a member of the Communist Party. In his autobiography, he dismisses the episode as prompted only by the 'far-fetched idea of gaining control [of the Oxford branch] and perhaps winning a free trip to Moscow or Leningrad'.[13] Yet one inevitably poses this incident against the dominant tone of the descriptions of his early life – the constant quest for the solution to boredom and to what he refers to on more than one occasion as manic depression. Without presuming to extrapolate too far from his brief published comments, it seems justified to assume that the Communist Party suggested for Greene, however briefly, a solution to his predicament. Disillusionment however was almost immediate, as he describes in *A Sort of Life*, and more effectively in the novel published in 1934, *It's a Battlefield*, which reflects both his attraction to and his final dissatisfaction with political commitment.

It's a Battlefield appeared in 1934, ten years after the passing encounter with the Communist Party. By this time he had been a convert to Roman Catholicism for eight years and opposition to a rival cause would have been an element in his antipathy. He had allied himself with a long conservative tradition against what many intellectuals saw as the hope for the future, and he felt the need to express his dissatisfaction with this newer faith. To write a novel at such a time pointing out the inadequacies of Communism as a belief was for a man of Greene's outlook a particularly courageous step; he did not conform to the popular equation of religion and reaction and has always been sympathetic to the cause of social justice. George

Orwell enthusiastically defended Greene against the charge of political reaction, taking his correspondent, T. R. Fyvel, to task. 'You keep referring to him as an extreme Conservative, the usual Catholic reactionary type. This isn't so at all, either in his books or privately. Of course he is a Catholic and in some issues he has to take sides politically with the Church, but in outlook he is just a mild Left with faint Communist Party leanings. I have even thought he might become our first Catholic fellow-traveller, a thing that doesn't exist in England.'[14] Greene himself has recently revealed that in fact he supported the Basque resistance to Franco, and had even attempted to persuade a cafe-owner in Toulouse to break the Nationalist blockade by flying him into Bilbao. In declaring at such a late date his opposition to Franco, he is still careful to avoid any implications of support for the Republicans; 'my sympathies were more engaged by the Catholic struggle against Franco than with the competing sectarians in Madrid'.[15] Greene's sympathies were with the Basques as Catholic revolutionaries, for revolution outside the auspices of the Church is in his eyes self-defeating. In *The Lawless Roads*, he describes how in Laredo, Texas, he became interested in a strike led by a local priest: 'This strike was the first example I had come across of genuine Catholic action on a social issue. . . . The intention was good, of course, but the performance was deplorable. You compared it mentally with the soap-box orator and the Red Flag and a crowd singing the Internationale. Catholicism, one felt, had got to rediscover the technique of revolution.'[16] The union of revolution and Catholicism is for Greene not only acceptable, but desirable. But Greene has an Orwellian horror of the world that the godless revolution will bring about, 'all gas-masks, tanks, and guns of a yet uninvented horror, a mechanistic world'.[17]

It's a Battlefield is Greene's most direct attempt to deal with the contemporary social and political atmosphere. His characters grasp at Communism not with the purity of idealists but as desperate, flawed people seeking escape from their social and psychological predicaments. Jim Drover, a quiet, unpresumptuous man, is arrested at a political demonstration after stabbing and killing a policeman for allegedly attacking his wife. He is sentenced to death, and a Party meeting is called to press for a reprieve. Greene's description of the meeting, though relentless, is certainly not the work of an inflexible anti-Communist, but of one who sympathizes with the need for belief, however unsatisfactory its object. 'Nobody', he wrote in *The Lawless Roads*, 'can endure existence without a philosophy.'[18] He conveys the aura of solidarity and purpose that pervades the hall as the meeting begins, 'the sincerity of the thousands who did not wrangle for leadership, who were ready to follow in patience and poverty'.[19] Greene's sympathies lie, sentimentally, with this amorphous body of people whose main characteristic is hope. When he focusses attentions on individuals, however, the meeting loses its spiritual quality. The revolutionary rhetoric of the fashionable intellectual, Mr Surrogate, stands in blatant contrast to his pampered life. He is in love with abstractions – 'Social Betterment, the Equality of Opportunity, the Means of Production' – and out of love with reality: 'In a cause was exhilaration, exaltation, a sense of Freedom; individuals gave pain by their brutality, their malice, their lack of understanding.'[20] It is this gap between the political ideal and the social fact that Greene consistently points to as the inevitable failure of secular commitment.

If other characters in the novel are treated more sympathetically, it is largely because they admit their own shaky bases for belief. For Conder, the journalist, Communism is merely one more component of a fantasy world in which he imagines himself now a respectable family man, now a director of Imperial Chemicals, and now a Red Crusader. It is one of the many masks he assumes to escape the reality of a bedsitter in Little Compton Street. Drover's brother Conrad is interested in the Party only in so far as it can help him to preserve the brother he idolizes. Kay Rimmer, though in her own way sympathetic to her brother-in-law and his probable fate, uses the Party mainly as a means of escaping temporarily the boredom of day to day existence; not for ideological reasons, but because at Communist Party meetings there are fifty men for every girl, a favourable ratio – 'art, politics, the church, Kay Rimmer had tried them all'.[21] Only Jules Briton is serious and explicit about what he would expect from Communism – 'he wanted something he could follow with passion'.[22] Jules is also a Catholic. Not much is made of this, but there are two important instances in which his religion is mentioned. He states mysteriously that 'none of you are going to do as much for Drover as I am. I feel it. None of you are going to do as much'.[23] Subsequently, in his 'home', the Church, Jules prays for Drover. It would be over-ingenious to suppose from this that Drover owes the eventual commutation of his sentence to a miracle, but the suggestion of a more powerful force than communism or political action is there. And when Jules contemplates marrying Kay Rimmer, it is important for him to know that she is a Catholic, for it makes the bearing of reality less hard, 'easier, then, the formality of marriage, more final the barrier against loneliness, an impregnable dyke till death; otherwise the sea corroded'.[24] These are the qualities Jules appreciates in his religion; he sees it as offering protection from the world. The Catholic sacrament of marriage, its guarantee of permanence rooted in the very essence of the Church, becomes for Jules a strangely negative consolation, a 'dyke' to hold back the flood of reality. Jules does not yield to the attractions of a political faith which claims – falsely for Greene – the power to change the order of things. Catholicism makes no such claim, but rather the power to justify and make significant the *present* order of things. From here, it is only a comparatively short step to Jules's notion of a Catholicism which makes life more 'bearable', and this is the level at which religion remains in the novel.

Greene felt the pull of Communism, the hold it had over intellectual life in the thirties, and over his generation in particular; but he could not believe in the possibility of a fair and just society because he had no corresponding belief in the essential goodness of man. Communism offered him no spiritual consolation for the oppressiveness of the world. It is just this consolation that Catholicism did offer. In an essay of 1936 on Henry James, Greene maintained that he had 'yet to find socialist or conservative who can feel any pity for the evil he denounces, and the final beauty of James's stories lies in their pity: "The poetry is in the pity."'[25] For Greene, any political belief involves the denunciation of a great part of human society, removing it beyond the bounds of sympathy. Political belief demands villains, and villains cannot be pitied. In political terms, pity is a weakness, but in terms of his religion, it is a sign of the individual's ability to accept the whole world, however sordid or oppressive, as part of God's design. Catholicism justifies the world as it is, not as it might be. In quoting the line of Wilfred Owen's, that 'the poetry is in the pity', Greene also emphasizes the connection between the ability to feel pity, and the expression of finer values in art. What is required of the artist is a willingness to understand and to sympathize. In Greene's view, the politically motivated writer denies sympathy to a large section of humanity, and is forced to take a blinkered view.

Greene looked to the present, not to what he regarded as an illusory future. 'There are others, of course, who prefer to look a stage ahead, for whom Intourist provides cheap tickets into a plausible future, but my journey represented a distrust of any future based on what we are.'[26] He scoffs at his contemporaries, but the description of his journey into the wilds of Liberia, recorded in *Journey Without Maps*, recalls the journeys undertaken by Upward and Warner's heroes, the journey of the single man through a frightening and

dangerous terrain in search of permanent values. Greene was particularly keen to observe in the primitive societies of Liberia the true
nature of humanity at its most basic level; to see, more clearly than
would be possible in a European, civilized society, the basic ignobility
of man. At the same time the tribal beliefs and rituals accorded this
ignoble existence value and dignity and significance; Liberia
appealed to him as a country in which the quotidian and the spiritual
were in obvious accord:

What is the fascination of this country on which the dead hand of the white
has never settled? I think it is a religious fascination: the country offers the
European an opportunity of living continuously in the presence of the
supernatural. The secret societies, as it were, sacramentalise the whole of
life.[27]

Greene uses the word 'religious' very much in the sense in which it is
used by Rex Warner, to describe the quality of significance and
permanence which both writers feel must lie beneath superficial
reality.

Christianity, as a possible alternative to the despair and futility of
contemporary existence, is present even in *England Made Me*, the
bleakest of Greene's thirties novels. The suggestion is conveyed
through the character of the decayed journalist Minty; out of the
desperate sordidness of his life, Minty feels the hope that the Church
may have to offer, but his approach is furtive and uncertain: 'A
church claimed him. The darkness, the glow of the sanctuary lamp
drew him more than food. It was Lutheran, of course, but it had the
genuine air of plaster images, of ever-burning light, of sins forgiven.
He looked this way and that, he bent his head and dived for the open
door, with the caution and dry mouthed excitement of a secret
debauchee.'[28] Minty senses the truth, but like Chant in *The Name of
Action* and Crane in *Rumour at Nightfall*, he cannot grasp it. There is in
this description of Minty's attraction to the Church a curious mixture
of authorial sympathy and contempt. The antithetical irony of the
phrase 'genuine air of plaster images' points to a failing in Minty's
understanding of Christianity and of God. His religion is superficial;
he regards it as a comforting retreat from the world, but has no
intellectual understanding of the nature of Christianity, and no
conception of its relation to contemporary society. Minty's idea of
God is of someone quite arbitrary in his actions; in the security of his
room Minty plays God with the life of a spider, keeping it imprisoned
under a tooth-glass. God is for Minty an omnipotent being who plays
with us for unfathomable reasons of his own, and in this sense

Minty's resort to the sanctuary of the Lutheran Church offers not hope but another version of despair.

Despite the noticeable change in Greene's fictional territory in the years from 1930 to 1935, from the early 'serious romances' to the contemporary realism of *It's a Battlefield* and *England Made Me*, there remains throughout a striking similarity in the descriptions of churches and in other references to religion. The church which seems to offer sanctuary to Minty is very like the church which offers temporary comfort to Oliver Chant in *The Name of Action*. Despite Greene's own declarations that his original commitment was intellectual rather than emotional, the comfort offered by religion in these novels is an emotional and sentimentalized one, powerful but undefined. At the same time there is the suggestion that Chant and Crane and Minty are attracted to religion for very personal reasons, and cannot see it as anything more than a means of personal salvation, a 'recipe for peace'. When Minty approaches the church with the 'dry mouthed excitement of a secret debauchee', he is clearly resorting to religion as a kind of drug, a magic potion that will make life easier for him. Only with *Brighton Rock* does Greene make religion, and specifically Catholicism, a central fact of contemporary life, understood by the hero as a belief with certain rules and certain demands. The previous novels appear to deny the contemporary validity of Catholicism, or at least of the kind of simplified, romanticized religion they describe; *Brighton Rock*, by contrast, attempts to justify it. In this sense, Greene's own view of the novel as a definite departure from earlier work becomes clearer.

Pinkie Brown is leader of a Brighton gang at seventeen, a cheat, a liar and a murderer. But Pinkie is also a Catholic, and his commitment is, as Greene claims of his own, based on reason:

'Of course it's true,' the boy said. 'What else could there be?' he went scornfully on. 'Why,' he said, 'it's the only thing that fits. These atheists, they don't know nothing. Of course there's Hell. Flames and damnation,' he said with his eyes on the dark shifting water and the lightning and the lamps going out above the black struts of the Palace Pier, 'torments'.[29]

The apparent logic of Pinkie's belief rests on the same paradox as Greene's own. The dialogue provides the reasoned assertion of Catholicism as 'the only thing that fits', but the accompanying description emphasizes the appropriateness of Pinkie's Catholicism to a pessimistic world-view that may be innate, or may be acquired, but is not necessarily logical. Reason, logic, intellect – such terms, commonly invoked in the thirties to justify belief, did not include in their range of definition the spirit of inquiry. The function of 'reason' is rather to reinforce and legitimize the instincts. Pinkie's confidence in the existence of hell, expressed in repeated 'of courses' only emphasizes how immensely important it is to him that hell should exist. For Pinkie there is no point in being merely bad, he must be evil. Anyone is capable of being bad, but the judgement of actions as good or bad, right or wrong, is for Greene and for Pinkie a purely arbitrary one, based upon values that have no solid support. It is impossible in Greene's terms to evaluate action if there is no creed upon which to base decisions; only belief can evaluate action. The best that may otherwise be relied upon is an instinctive knowledge of right and wrong, which is in fact little more than a series of prejudices accumulated over a lifetime. Ida Arnold, pursuing Pinkie in the name of her own concept of justice, bases her actions upon personal, arbitrary values, and is thus condemned. For Greene, the qualities she possesses are negative ones – she is a good sort; her virtues, such as they are, exist in a vacuum. When Ida resolves to pursue the murderer of the man who has been kind to her, she is relying solely on her own judgement. In Greene's terms, she is adopting deliberately the role of fate, and this is presumptuous, misplaced righteousness. She assumes the task of retribution with an inadequate set of values to support her. The text consistently denigrates Ida Arnold's virtues; her kindness is 'Guiness kindness'. Greene plays deliberately upon conventional notions of natural justice by describing them as perverse and self-indulgent, whereas Pinkie's actions, which are in terms of conventional morality reprehensible, are also morally superior by dint of his belief in Catholicism.

Pinkie's actions, however anti-human, are based on a set of prescribed values. He believes in the evil of his deeds, and that they will lead him certainly to damnation. He is thus able to place his temporal actions in a wider context, and to discover for himself the importance of actions which would be otherwise insignificant. They are made significant by the certainty of the punishment he will receive from a higher authority than Ida Arnold. In the face of God and Evil, Ida's concept of right and wrong seems not to matter:

'There's things you don't know.' Rose brooded darkly by the bed, while [Ida Arnold] argued on: a God wept in a garden and cried out upon a cross. . . .

'I know one thing you don't. I know the difference between Right and Wrong. They didn't teach you *that* at school.'

Rose didn't answer; the woman was quite right; the two words meant nothing to her. Their taste was extinguished by stronger foods – Good and

Evil. The woman could tell her nothing she didn't know about these – she knew by tests as clear as mathematics that Pinkie was evil – what did it matter in that case whether he was right or wrong.[30]

Unlike Ida Arnold, Pinkie shares Greene's pessimistic world view. A weary assertion from Rose that 'life's not so bad', prompts from Pinkie a vehement reply: 'Don't you believe it,' he said, 'I'll tell you what it is. It's gaol, it's not knowing where to get some money. Worms and cataract, cancer. You hear 'em shrieking from the upper windows – children being born. It's dying slowly.'[31] Pinkie's jaundiced view is made to carry a great deal more weight than the Rose-coloured. Our unconsidered notions of what is to be admired and what condemned, what is sympathetic and what unsympathetic, are reversed in *Brighton Rock*. Or are they? Waugh plays upon complacent notions of moral good in *Black Mischief* in order to point up their superficiality. But in Waugh's description of Seth's birth control campaign, we are actually allowed to share Seth's assumptions, so that the condemnation of Seth is a condemnation of the reader's complacency. Greene also evokes a conventional notion of goodness, Ida Arnold's, in order to condemn it, but in *Brighton Rock* the text distances the reader from Ida. We do not discover for ourselves as it were that we have been mistaken, our sympathy with her misplaced. Instead it is always clear she is on the wrong side, despite her obsession with natural justice. Greene establishes Pinkie's moral superiority by appealing to another kind of complacency in the reader, by which the positive is accepted as the superficial, and the negative as the profound. Pinkie's stylized world of dark passions and expressionist lighting is founded as securely on sentimentality as Ida's drunken bonhomie. His authority in the novel depends upon a superficial acceptance by the reader of the profundity of his vision.

The acts Pinkie commits may be defined according to the individual perspective as cruel, bad, anti-social, defiant; but according to the perspective of Roman Catholicism they are evil. Pinkie has committed and continues to commit mortal sin. Given this, it would seem at first that his actions involve a kind of courage of commitment, a resolve to act and to accept the consequences, were it not made clear that Pinkie's personality is a fixed result of his environment. As such the murders of Hale and Dallow, the cynical marriage to Rose, would have taken place regardless of his religious beliefs. They may have been in Greene's terminology merely wrong, but they would still have occurred. It is a paradox therefore that Pinkie's awareness of his own future damnation should render his actions not harder to live with, but easier. Pinkie's Catholicism does not dictate individual action, but dignifies acts already committed. In this sense Greene's understanding of the relationship between faith and action differs from that of the revolutionary novelists. Both Warner and Upward regard revolutionary action as an accumulation of individual acts each of which is undertaken as a contribution to the revolution. It is true that the most mundane acts gain significance from the actor's belief in revolutionary socialism, but there are also a large number of acts – joining the Party, making contact with the workers, spreading the message of revolution – that would not otherwise have been undertaken. By contrast, there is no suggestion in *Brighton Rock* that belief in Catholicism genuinely influences action – its important function is to change the light by which the value of action is seen and judged. All acts are transformed by the rules of the Church into significant acts – Pinkie's wrongdoing assumes some meaning in the wider scheme of things. It is in this sense that Greene's novel is, as he claims, an examination of 'the effect of faith on action'. The certainty of Hell provided by Pinkie's religious belief lends purpose to the crimes he was predestined to commit.

Pinkie cannot bear the idea that his existence may be pointless. The conscious progress towards Hell gives him the knowledge of his own significance that he requires. He acts within a strictly defined framework of divine reward and punishment. Pinkie's lot will be punishment, but that is preferable for him to the knowledge that whatever his temporal actions, the end result will be a vacuum. The prospect of damnation offers eventual escape from the reality he detests, for life appals Pinkie: 'She got up and he saw the skin of her thigh for a moment above the artificial silk, and a prick of sexual desire disturbed him like a sickness. That was what happened to a man in the end: the stuffy room, the wakeful children, the Saturday night movements from the other bed. Was there no escape – any-where – for anyone?'[32] To escape all this, Pinkie uses his inherited Catholicism in a very calculating sense. Not only does it lend his actions significance, but in a logical way it justifies them, for murder and betrayal are leading him surely out of the unbearable world he inhabits, if only to Hell. 'It was worth murdering a world.'[33] Even so, Pinkie's commitment to damnation cannot be total, for it is not simply in damnation but in Catholicism that he places his faith. He must believe, however half-heartedly, in the *possibility* of salvation. He remembers as a kind of talisman part of the familiar quotation from William Camden's 'Epitaphs', which reads more fully:

'My friend judge not me,
Thou seest I judge not thee:
Betwixt the stirrup and the ground,
Mercy I asked, mercy I found.'[34]

When Rose, the pathetic bride-to-be, asks Pinkie if he believes in 'it', he answers with conviction that of course there is a Hell: '"And Heaven too," Rose said with anxiety, while the rain fell interminably on. "Oh, maybe," the Boy said, "maybe."'[35] Pinkie has to believe in Heaven as the mirror image of his own goal, but there is a weary obligation about it. If he believes intellectually in the logic and fitness of eternal damnation, he is forced by his religious faith to hold a similar belief in eternal reward. The difference for Pinkie is that while his emotions, his very existence, support the belief in damnation, there is no corresponding support for salvation. To repent would be to deny the significance of his own existence, for if the simple act of repentance could wipe out his crimes, then the structure and purpose he had given them by his faith in religion would disappear as well. For Pinkie, confirmation of the significance of his temporal existence will come only when he is made to suffer eternally for it.

Despite the dominant movement of the novel towards this end, Greene does, in the last few pages, reassert the possibility of salvation implied earlier in the lines from Camden. After Pinkie's plan to trick Rose into committing suicide has been thwarted, and he has been killed instead, Rose seeks the comfort of the confessional. Here, in this final scene, Mary McCarthy's charge that Greene is an 'ersatz serious novelist'[36] seems inescapable. The old priest's words, implying a comparison between Pinkie and Péguy, are unconvincing. Pinkie may have been in a state of mortal sin, but not because, like Péguy, 'he couldn't bear the idea that any soul could suffer damnation'.[37] Pinkie revels in the idea. Perhaps, though, these lines apply to Rose, for she cannot bear the thought of Pinkie in Hell, and wants to be damned herself that she may be with him. But the homily delivered at the end of the priest's speech seems to refer to Pinkie: 'You can't conceive, my child, nor can I or anyone . . . the . . . appalling strangeness of the mercy of God.'[38] It is Rose's rejoinder that convinces: 'He's damned. He knew what he was about.'[39] The internal logic of the novel leads towards Pinkie's damnation, but commitment to damnation is not regarded by Greene as its own justification; it is instead the discernible evidence of commitment to Catholicism. The conscious progress towards eternal punishment must include the faith in all aspects of religion, including the possibility of salvation. Just as T. S. Eliot regarded Baudelaire's deliberate 'capacity for damnation'[40] as leaving the way open for salvation, so Greene saw, in the conscious evil of Baron Corvo, 'the potential sanctity of the man'.[41] It is not by any means an unfamiliar argument, that the perpetrator of evil acts is afforded the chance of heavenly forgiveness, whereas the Ida Arnolds of the world, who are unaware of the distinction between good and evil, have not even this slim chance. Yet at the end of *Brighton Rock*, Greene seems unwilling to leave the affirmation of the novel to rest upon an implied and comparatively sophisticated theological argument, and so Rose is pregnant. The emphasis is taken off Pinkie's apparent damnation and put onto the future. There will be a baby, and Rose, if she survives the horror of the recording Pinkie has bequeathed her, may 'make him a saint – to pray for his father'.[42] Pinkie's damnation is by no means complete. But the possibility of salvation also implies the negation of Pinkie, for salvation would render his temporal actions – his entire life – insignificant.

The provisos that Greene attaches to Pinkie's damnation smack very much of the sentimentality which he condemned elsewhere as a 'pernicious influence' on literature.[43] Reviewing Chaplin's *Modern Times*, he objected to the 'unfair pathos of the blind girl and the orphan child,'[44] but in *Brighton Rock* he is not above a little unfair pathos of his own. The references to Camden's lines, and to Péguy, are an attempt to offer hope for Pinkie's soul, but the momentum of Pinkie's progress towards damnation is too great to be broken by a pair of academic niceties. And so Greene allows the weight of the ending to rest upon a child. The unresolved complexities of the argument he has constructed are shunted into the hazy future, and sentimentality triumphs over logic, emotion over reason. So despite Greene's contempt for the Communist writer's faith in a Utopian future, the ending of *Brighton Rock* suggests a similar confidence. Belief not only justifies present action, it also offers the possibility of eventual reward – salvation – for having acted as a believer. During a conversation recorded in Paris in 1950 for the Catholic journal *Dieu Vivant*, Greene rather confused his interlocutors by assuring them that contrary to all their assumptions, Pinkie is indeed saved at the end. But, they persisted, you seem in the novel to give in to the blackest pessimism. 'Pessimiste, moi!' Greene replied. 'Je me croyais au contraire débordant d'optimisme.'[45] Behind the relentless cynicism of *Brighton Rock* – the ignobility and the seediness, the emphasis on evil and damnation – are optimism and confidence and faith, all of which lie beyond logical justification.

NOTES

1. 'Introduction' *Brighton Rock* (1970) pp. vii–ix.
2. *Journey Without Maps* (1935) p. 5.
3. 'Come Inside' *The Road to Damascus* ed. J. A. O'Brien (1949) p. 16.
4. *A Sort of Life* p. 165.
5. 'Introduction' *Brighton Rock* p. vii.
6. Willis, 'New Life for the Novel' p. 14.
7. Philip Toynbee, 'Literature and Life . . .' *Observer* (15.9.57) p. 3.
8. 'Introduction' *Brighton Rock* p. viii.
9. *The Name of Action* (1930) p. 169.
10. Ibid p. 283.
11. Ibid p. 291.
12. *Rumour at Nightfall* (1931) pp. 129–30.
13. *A Sort of Life* p. 132.
14. 'Letter to T. R. Fyvel' (15.4.49) *Essays* 4 p. 496.
15. 'Introduction' *Brighton Rock* p. ix.
16. *The Lawless Roads* pp. 28–9.
17. Ibid.
18. Ibid p. 272.
19. *It's a Battlefield* (1934) p. 52.
20. Ibid p. 57.
21. Ibid p. 32.
22. Ibid p. 47.
23. Ibid p. 184.
24. Ibid p. 201.
25. 'Henry James . . .' *Collected Essays* p. 38.
26. *Journey Without Maps* p. 9.
27. 'Three Travellers' *Spectator* 163 (8.12.39) p. 838.
28. *England Made Me* (1935) p. 132.
29. *Brighton Rock* (1938) p. 71.
30. Ibid p. 289.
31. Ibid p. 330.
32. Ibid pp. 127–8.
33. Ibid p. 128.
34. *Remains Concerning Britain* (1870) p. 420.
35. *Brighton Rock* p. 71.
36. 'Graham Greene and the Intelligentsia' *Partisan Review* 11 (Spring 1944) p. 229.
37. *Brighton Rock* p. 359.
38. Ibid.
39. Ibid p. 360.
40. 'Baudelaire' (1930) *Selected Essays* (1951) p. 429.
41. 'Frederick Rolfe . . .' (1935) *Collected Essays* p. 181.
42. *Brighton Rock* p. 360.
43. *Lord Rochester's Monkey* (1974) p. 186. Written 'around 1931 to 1934'.
44. 'Modern Times' (1936) *The Pleasure Dome* (1972) p. 51.
45. Père Jouve and Marcel Moré, 'Propos de table avec Graham Greene' *Dieu Vivant* 16 (1950) p. 129.

Chapter 5

The Catholic Novelist II:
Evelyn Waugh

Evelyn Waugh's conversion to Catholicism in 1930 neatly divides the two decades: the aestheticism and frivolity of the twenties give way to the new seriousness of the thirties. The pleasing symmetry of this judgement does however obscure the fact that Waugh had from an early age shown a marked religious temperament, and at school passed through a fairly conventional period of adolescent piety. He became convinced during his last year at school that he was in fact an atheist, but religion was not entirely dismissed from his mind during the following years. The diaries covering the twenties contain a number of references to Catholicism, dating from the conversion in 1924 of his great friend Alastair Graham, in which flippancy betrays a genuine interest. And in the entry for 22 December 1925 he records how he 'sat up until 7 in the morning arguing about the Roman Church'.[1] Waugh later recalled that he had lost his early, childhood faith as the result of what he took to be rational arguments,[2] and according to his religious instructor, Father Martin D'Arcy, 'what reason had taken away, reason had to bring back. . . . Evelyn never liked the heart to sidetrack reason or serve as a substitute. On the other hand, the heart's desire, the cry of the innermost self, could ally itself to reason and set him on the quest for a Holy Grail. . . . It is this special kind of combination of a sick self, bored with and feeding on emptiness, and a hard brain, which prevented him from being taken in by the popular idols.'[3] Father D'Arcy discusses Waugh's progress towards commitment in the language of the thirties; his argument is an elegant rationalization of an implied conflict between the 'intellectual' and the 'emotional' motivations towards belief. D'Arcy does not, as Waugh and Graham Greene both at various times tried to do, deny the emotional element, the 'heart's desire', altogether; instead he resolves any possible conflict between a belief which appeals to the heart, and a belief which appeals to the brain, by regarding Catholicism as the only belief capable of satisfying both.

Christopher Sykes perceives in the despair and ennui expressed by Waugh in the early twenties not just youthful affectation, but a 'deep-rooted distress'.[4] Along with other writers of his generation, he was acutely conscious of something missing from modern life that had once been present; what Greene calls the 'religious sense', and Warner the 'mystery' of life, Waugh refers to as 'the beauty of living', which he felt had 'gone out of the youngest generation'.[5] The beauty of living for which the young Waugh longed was partly a sense of purpose, of participating importantly in a society which itself possessed confidence. For Waugh, as for others, that kind of society disappeared with the First World War, and with it went the possibility of significant action. Waugh and his generation could not hope to emulate Rupert Brooke, who seemed, with his beauty and his talent and his death, to embody everything of which they had been cheated. Waugh recorded the envy he felt when reading Brooke's letters, 'particularly the parts about Rugby and friendship. I do honestly think that this is something that went out of the world in 1914, at least for one generation.'[6] As something went out of the world, so came the desire for something to replace it, what Waugh called the desire 'to merge one's individual destiny in forces outside oneself'.[7] In 1929, his style by then prematurely old, Waugh lamented 'the fundamental failing of the whole of the younger generation – that is their almost complete lack of any qualitative standards'.[8] In the word 'standards' can be glimpsed the vital attraction of Catholicism for Waugh. It appeared as a constant and immutable set of values by which the world and the individual's place within it could be irrefutably defined. He was by 1929 consciously dissociating himself from his own lost generation, and taking on the colours of the believer. It was a step he took very seriously. His first travel book, *Labels*, published in 1930 contains irreverent remarks about Catholicism which Waugh felt himself obliged to disown in an author's note: 'So far as this book contains any serious opinions, they are those of the dates with which it deals, eighteen months ago. Since then my views of several subjects, and particularly on Roman Catholicism, have developed and changed in many ways.'[9]

There are a number of references to Catholicism in Waugh's fiction of the thirties, and it is worth noticing that specifically Catholic characters such as Father Rothschild in *Vile Bodies* stand outside the main focus of his satirical range. But on only one occasion is Catholicism explicitly presented as a source of permanent values and as the means by which we order our lives, in his short story 'Out of Depth'. The hero, Rip Van Winkle, awakes five hundred years hence to a London in which the white inhabitants are ruled by a race of dark-skinned invaders. Waugh clearly intended this as a startling and shocking inversion. Lost in this upside-down world, Rip, a Catholic, does at last find solace in 'something that was new yet ageless':

The word 'Mission' painted on a board; a black man dressed as a Dominican friar . . . and a growing clearness. Rip knew that out of the strangeness, there had come into being something familiar; a shape in chaos. Something was being done that Rip knew; something that twenty-five centuries had not altered; of his own childhood which survived that age of the world. In a log-built church at the coast town he was squatting among a native congregation; some of them in cast-off uniforms; the women had shapeless, convent-sewn frocks; all around him dishevelled white men were staring ahead with vague, uncomprehending eyes, to the end of the room where two candles burned. The priest turned towards them his bland, black face.

'Ite, missa est.'[10]

Waugh describes the ceremony of the mass as 'a shape in chaos', and nowhere in his fiction of the thirties does his notion of the function of Catholicism emerge with such clarity. Catholicism is the one thing to have survived from the old world, enabling Rip to comprehend and to come to terms with his predicament, and to find consolation. The implication is that Catholicism explains and makes coherent not only the contemporary social reality, but all conceivable realities. This story first appeared in 1933, and in January of that year Waugh had been severely vilified in the established Catholic journal *The Tablet* – apropos of his recently published *Black Mischief* – for neglecting his duties as a Catholic writer. Considering the lack of young Catholic novelists willing to come to grips with the thirties, it might seem that Waugh's conversion, after the popular success of his first novel, would have been welcomed by the Catholic press, and an effort made to assimilate his satirical style. On the contrary, the Editor of *The Tablet* branded Waugh as a traitor to his new faith.[11] Twelve of Waugh's Catholic friends and admirers signed a letter protesting *The Tablet*'s action.[12] A lengthy correspondence was initiated, and *The Tablet* provided with the opportunity to condemn the novel further. After six weeks of argument in their columns, the subject was finally closed by the magazine's announcement of a new translation of the Instructions of the Holy Office on immodest books.[13]

This would be an interesting but insignificant episode, were it not for Waugh's lengthy open letter to the Archbishop of Westminster, which has remained unpublished, in which he responded in detail to the charges laid against him by *The Tablet*. The letter indicates that he was greatly disturbed and upset by the incident, in particular the suggestion that he did not deserve the name of Catholic. Quoting the original notice in *The Tablet*, he submits to the Archbishop (as legal proprietor of the paper) that 'no charge could be more odious than the one contained in this paragraph nor, if unfounded, more grossly scurrilous'. Beneath his often witty contempt for the level of attack, there is an element of uneasiness over his exact duties as a public convert:

The Editor of [The] *Tablet* remarks that he does not know whether I still consider myself a Catholic, and it occurs to me that the suspicion that I do not, may arrive less from my book, than from the fact that frequently during the last two years I have excused myself from participating in various laudable undertakings, have not spoken or exhibited myself on Catholic platforms, and have declined some invitations with which I have been honoured by Catholic Leagues and Associations.

   The path of a convert in England is not without its embarrassments. There are some who throw themselves generously into every kind of public work, lecturing to societies, serving on committees, giving unmistakable testimony in every moment of their conversation to the Faith they have received; these are often too rewarded with a slightly supercilious amusement by old Catholics. Others, of whom I am one, prefer to perform their religious duties without ostentation, to lead a normal life in the world and earn their living in what seems to them an honourable fashion.[14]

Waugh reveals himself as reluctant to adopt the conventional convert's role. He fears association with the duller, workaday aspects of the Church, and exposure to the 'supercilious amusement' of born Catholics. At the same time he is at pains to establish that he has in no way offended the Church during the practice of his 'trade' as a novelist. The balance of his attitude is contained in a short passage in which he points out 'that the only wholly admirable character [in *Black Mischief*] is the only Catholic, a White Father missionary, and the only wholly contemptible one a militant Free-Mason atheist; but that is beside the point. It is not required of me to prove that mine is an actively propagandist work.'[15] As a novelist he would ensure that all references to Catholicism were favourable, but he could not undertake directly to further the cause. By doing so he would be sacrificing artistic subtlety for the blatancy of propaganda. It is a reasonable argument, but the tone is defensive, suggesting a genuine uncertainty on Waugh's part over the relationship of art and belief. Catholicism is only marginally present in the fiction before *Brideshead Revisited*; despair, rather than the consolations of religious faith, dominates his thirties work. Waugh went some way towards explaining his failure to apply the 'standards' of Catholicism to his fictional universe when he remarked of *A Handful of Dust* (1934) that it 'contained all that I had to say about humanism'.[16] He seemed to see his novels of the thirties, in retrospect, as an indictment of humanism, of the individual's efforts to seek fulfilment in personal relationships or in anything purely temporal.

This belief that man alone could achieve nothing combined smoothly with Waugh's political conservatism. The question of how far his conservatism can be viewed as a genuinely political stance is more difficult. Christopher Sykes begins his biography of Waugh by dismissing his political beliefs as archaic, cranky, and 'utterly ridiculous',[17] but there is evidence which, while hardly conclusive, does suggest that Waugh's political attitudes in the thirties were consciously relevant to the issues of the time. His well-known reply to the *Left Review* questionnaire on the Spanish Civil War places him as a fairly typical right-wing conservative of the thirties, rather than as a political eccentric:

> I know Spain only as a tourist and a reader of newspapers. I am no more impressed by the 'legality' of the Valencia government than are English Communists by the legality of the Crown, Lords, and Commons. I believe it was a bad government, rapidly deteriorating. If I were a Spaniard, I would be fighting for General Franco. As an Englishman I am not in the predicament of choosing between two evils. I am not a Fascist nor shall I become one unless it were the only alternative to Marxism. It is mischievous to suggest that such a choice is imminent.[18]

Nor was his support of Franco and the Insurgents purely hypothetical, for in September of 1936 he records having attended a 'meeting of the Archbishop's Spanish Association'.[19] Waugh's conservative sympathies emerge too in his attitude to the Abyssinian crisis. Because of his knowledge of and interest in Abyssinia, gained on his first African journey in 1930, Waugh subsequently made two trips in 1935 and 1936 to record his impressions for the right-wing *Daily Mail*. The result, *Waugh in Abyssinia* (1936), makes obvious his support for the invading Italians. He refuses to regard the Abyssinians in conventional liberal terms, as a noble people cruelly used. Instead he draws attention to the barbarity of the Ethiopian tribes and to the profound divisions in a nation of people thrown together by accidents of geography and tribal warfare. It is ironical that Waugh, who spoke out so eloquently against the sterility of the twenties and thirties, should here show a disconcerting admiration for the forces of technology as personified by the Italians, and a corresponding contempt for the desperate bungling of the Abyssinians. Against the prevailing intellectual mood of the time, but by no means out of step with public opinion, Waugh regarded the Italian invasion as justified by the laws of Imperialism.

In his last travel book of the thirties, *Robbery Under Law*, Waugh justified his conservative views with deliberate reasonableness:

A conservative is not merely an obstructionist who wishes to resist the introduction of novelties; nor is he, as was assumed by most nineteenth-century parliamentarians, a brake to frivolous experiment. He has positive work to do. . . . Civilization has no force of its own beyond what is given it from within. It is under constant assault and it takes most of the energies of civilized man to keep going at all. There are criminal ideas and a criminal class in every nation and the first action of every revolution, figuratively and literally, is to open the prisons. Barbarism is never finally defeated; given propitious circumstances, men and women who seem quite orderly, will commit every conceivable atrocity. The danger does not come merely from habitual hooligans; we are all potential recruits for anarchy. Unremitting effort is needed to keep men living together at peace. . . .[20]

Behind Waugh's conservative philosophy is the conviction that the natural propensity of mankind is anarchy and disorder. But alongside this conventional conservatism stood a contempt for all institutions and his paradoxical attraction towards those individuals, such as Margot Beste-Chetwynde and Basil Seal, whose very vitality and attractiveness springs from their defiance – within limitations – of conventional notions of order and propriety. This kind of conservatism, which combines respect for class and convention with sympathy for the reprobate and the bohemian is by no means uncommon, nor even as paradoxical as it may first appear. Margot Beste-Chetwynde and Basil Seal are free to break certain rules, but only because they conform to other, more subtle ones; Margot may be beyond the reach of the law, but her style is unimpeachable. Waugh's particular kind of conservatism allowed him to subscribe to the political attitudes which he outlined in *Robbery Under Law*, and at the same time retain a profound contempt for the general subject of 'politics'. In contrast to the political opinions seriously expressed in *Waugh in Abyssinia*, his fictional version of the crisis, *Scoop* (1938), dismisses all factions. Politics are reduced to the level of schoolboy games, with no serious claims upon the ideals. The huge family of Jacksons who run the country, and the menacing Dr Benito who establishes for one day the Soviet Union of Ishmaelia, are all seen as equally self-serving and are treated with equal disrespect. There are then two aspects to Waugh's political outlook; on the one hand, a fairly conventional right-wing conservatism which led to unremarkable stands on major issues, and on the other hand, a deep-seated contempt for politics as one of the games played by men. He deemed it 'futile to attempt to impose any kind of theological consistency in politics, which are not an exact science but, by their nature, a series of makeshift, rule-of-thumb, practical devices for getting out of scrapes'.[21] The adjective 'theological' is a resonant one. Waugh was contemptuous of any attempt to raise politics to the status of a belief, with immutable rules and values. A belief is by nature 'theological'; such consistency, in other words, may be found only in religion.

Waugh objected bitterly to those among his contemporaries who, in his view, attempted this very task – to impose upon a political, and therefore pragmatic outlook, a 'theological consistency'. *De haut en bas* he proclaimed the futility of political commitment and the essential absurdity of politics. This refusal to be taken in by what Father D'Arcy calls the 'popular idols' did not altogether prevent the indulgence in sentimentality. The notion of Waugh as quite resistant to political humbug can be usefully balanced by an incident from *Remote People*, in which he spends some time amongst the expatriate planters in Kenya. In contrast to his usual detached and dismissive tone, Waugh waxes lyrical over the settlers' way of life, and fatuously includes them in an idealized squirearchical tradition, as the direct descendants of the hard-drinking, fair-dealing landowners of eighteenth-century England. Waugh was attracted to the idea of an élite, who by some undefined means were singled out as spiritually superior to their fellows, who did not live by the same rules as ordinary people. His first novel, *Decline and Fall*, attempts a justification of this notion.

In *Decline and Fall* Waugh appears on the one hand to speak from a conventional conservatism. Though Margot Beste-Chetwynde moves in Society, her origins are obscure and she has no feeling for that traditional base of the upper classes which stands for 'something enduring and serene in a world that had lost its reason'.[22] Her country house, the finest example of domestic Tudor architecture in England, is summarily razed to make way for 'something clean and square'. But the opposition between the values of tradition and the insensitivity of the *parvenu* is not a simple one, for Waugh also suggests that Margot may have other, more significant qualifications entitling her to membership of an elect. When Paul Pennyfeather is sent to prison, for crimes of which he is innocent and Margot guilty, he is compensated by his confidence in 'doing the right thing'. This confidence is not however based on social convention or inherited morality. Paul indeed questions the 'whole code of ready-made honour that is the still small voice trained to command of the Englishmen all the world over', and instead finds justification for the sacrificial act in the character of Margot. 'As he studied Margot's photograph, dubiously transmitted as it was, he was strengthened in his belief that there was, in fact, and should be, one law for her and another for himself, and that the raw little exertions of nineteenth-century Radicals were essentially base and trivial and misdirected.'[23] When Paul accepts the impossibility of Margot in prison, he is rejecting conventional morality, rejecting as inadequate both the gentlemanly code in which he has been educated, and the humanist inheritance from those 'raw little . . . nineteenth-century Radicals'. He can offer no other moral system to replace them, but retains nevertheless the instinctive conviction that there is something else, some justification for his innate certainty of Margot's unaccountability. It is the feeling that permeates the thirties generation, that the inherited accretion of rules by which we evaluate our conduct is without weight or conviction. In *Decline and Fall*, Waugh in effect poses two possible means of evaluating action. His opposition is crude, and its implications barely explored, but the basic division is clear: two kinds of judgements may be made, the judgements of right and wrong based on social convention, which apply to and are applied by the vast majority of ordinary people, and the judgements of right and wrong which apply to those few who can be regarded as in some sense superior. Waugh's distinction is an embryonic form of the distinction Greene drew ten years later in *Brighton Rock*.

The division is between the great mass of people and the chosen few who are awarded, by undescribed means, a kind of spiritual superiority. This suggestion in *Decline and Fall* of a superior category of humanity, who see themselves and the world differently, is thus present in Waugh's writing two years before his conversion to Catholicism. In *Brideshead Revisited*, published seventeen years later, Sebastian attempts to explain how Catholics are different from ordinary people. He echoes the language of *Decline and Fall*; 'they've got an entirely different outlook on life; everything they think important, is different from other people'.[24] Catholicism is here offered as the justification for, the secure basis of, the distinction first posed in *Decline and Fall*. Belief in Catholicism affords the individual access to a system of rules and means of evaluation different in kind from those available to the unbeliever. The exact quality of this difference in kind is not clear from *Decline and Fall*, but is specified in *Brideshead Revisited*. For the Catholic believer everything is different because through his Catholicism he has been granted the true understanding of reality. The Beste-Chetwyndes and the Marchmains are both described as belonging to special, smaller categories of humanity, in which they judge and are judged by different rules. The hero in both novels is thus confronted by characters who possess a certainty of their own function and significance not provided by the conventional, humanistic code to which the hero subscribes. In *Brideshead Revisited*, because the basis of this certainty is specified as Catholicism, Charles Ryder accordingly abandons his scepticism and becomes a convert, in order to attain the certainty and spiritual status for himself. But in *Decline and Fall*, this spiritual distinction is merely presented as a mysterious fact of life – one is either 'static' like Paul, or 'dynamic' like Margot, and the categorization is inescapable. In a conversation with Peter Beste-Chetwynde at the end of the novel, Paul accepts his lot: 'You know, Paul, I think it was a mistake you ever got mixed up with us; don't you? We're different somehow. Don't quite know how. Don't think that's rude, do you, Paul?' 'No, I know exactly what you mean. You're dynamic, and I'm static.'[25] In the opposite but to some extent complementary personalities of Peter and Paul, Waugh explores the possibilities of the individual's relationship to his society. Despite the clear attraction that Waugh feels for the glamour and decadence of the Beste-Chetwyndes, no simple authorial judgements are being made. Paul returns to a conventional life, but he is by no means condemned for this. He comes to recognize that the certainty and confidence, the 'dynamism' of Peter Beste-Chetwynde, is as precarious as any conventional morality, because it has no firm basis. The security of faith that supports the Marchmains is unavailable to the Beste-Chetwyndes. In the fates of Peter and Paul can be seen the alternative fates that seemed, in Waugh's eyes, to face the young man of the thirties generation. He could, like Paul, accept the inevitability of self-limitation and insignificance, or he could, like Peter, place himself outside convention, only to come adrift.

The notion of a spiritual elect, distinguishable simply by their vitality and *sang-froid*, is already being questioned in *Decline and Fall* itself. Vitality is not its own justification, and in *Vile Bodies* Waugh sees it as facile and purposeless. Adam Fenwick-Symes acts out with his sometime fiancée Nina a series of farcical exchanges in which their engagement is made and broken according to Adam's fluctuating financial prospects. Beneath lies both a wariness of emotional commitment, and a developing desire for it:

> Nina: 'Darling, I *am* glad about our getting married.'
> Adam: 'So am I. But don't let's get intense about it.'[26]

When Nina confesses a kind of relief at the thought of marrying, she is breaking their flimsy social rules and stands corrected by Adam. Marriage and love are 'static', the refuges of the insignificant. But on the other hand they offer the security and purpose so avidly sought by the thirties generation. Amidst the turmoil of one of their 'original' parties, Adam confesses to Nina that he is seeking some sort of permanence, perhaps that offered by marriage:

'. . . I don't know if it sounds absurd,' said Adam, 'but I do feel that a marriage ought to *go on* – for quite a long time, I mean. D'you feel that too, at all?' 'I'm glad you feel that. I didn't quite know if you did. Otherwise it's all rather bogus, isn't it?'[27]

This attitude to marriage runs through the fiction of the thirties generation. There is a consciousness that marriage has become just a social convention, but at the same time there is a desire to re-assert the significance of marriage. For Waugh and Greene, Catholicism declared marriage an irrevocable sacrament and thus a guarantee of permanence, but even non-Catholic novelists invested marriage with something of this sacramental significance. Rex Warner and George Orwell both emphasize the sanctity of marriage, as though endowing a conventional institution with the force and authority it once possessed. Rather like George in *The Wild Goose Chase* or Gordon in *Keep the Aspidistra Flying*, Adam requires that marriage be not just a social convention, but a significant act, affirming his own significance. 'Otherwise it's all rather bogus.' This desire for permanence and significance is expressed quite clearly by Father Rothschild, whose unlikely name does not detract from the essential seriousness of his observation: 'I don't think people ever *want* to lose their faith either in religion or anything else. I know very few young people, but it seems to me that they are all possessed with an almost fatal hunger for permanence. I think all these divorces show that. People aren't content just to muddle along nowadays . . . And this word "bogus" they all use. . . . They won't make the best of a bad job nowadays.'[28] The phrase 'an almost fatal hunger for permanence' captures all the earnestness and portentousness that lies not far below the satire. *Decline and Fall* and *Vile Bodies* together come to an exploration, largely but not exclusively comic, of the possibilities of permanence. But none of these possibilities can hold off the threat of chaos. World war descends at the end of *Vile Bodies*, and the hero finds himself in an unrecognizable world, a world with which he has no significant connection whatsoever, 'a great expanse of mud in which every visible object was burnt or broken'.[29]

The predicament of the hero in a world without meaningful values is a major concern of *Decline and Fall*, *Vile Bodies*, and *Black Mischief*, but it was not until 1934 and the publication of *A Handful of Dust* that

Waugh approached the subject with any real rigour. In the terminology of *Decline and Fall*, Tony Last is a 'static' character. He is very
much a thirties hero, lacking the energy that Waugh found so attractive in the Bright Young Things. Like Paul Pennyfeather, he is an
ordinary man, completely at the mercy of events. He puts his faith in
tradition and the land and his family, and when they fail him turns
not to the consolations of the social whirl but to an elaborate version
of the romantic quest. He does not find the object of his quest, for
within the humanistic limitations that Waugh imposes on the novel
he cannot. Authorial sympathy is with him however because he
makes the attempt. At the beginning of the novel, life for Tony seems
ideal. Everything is regular and ordered. His bedroom, littered with
the relics of childhood and adolescence, is an embodiment of stability.
The very names of the rooms at Hetton suggest the illusoriness of this
stability, a childhood preserved beyond its span; Guinevere, Galahad,
Morgan le Fay. Tony places his child-like faith in things unable to
bear the weight. Marriage, which suggests the possibility of permanence in *Vile Bodies*, has become in *A Handful of Dust* simply
another inadequate human relationship. Brenda is a 'nereid' from
another domain, and no significant contact is possible.

Tony's other bulwark, his faith in the past, has as its logical coun-
terpart a faith in the future – or rather in the continuation of that past
into the indefinite future. He can believe in such continuity because
of his son, whose existence guarantees Tony's spiritual presence at
Hetton even after his death. But he does not count on other laws
which have little regard for the requirements of heredity. The difficulty comes in understanding these other laws, and by what logic
they operate. The accident in which the boy is killed is, it is emphasized, 'nobody's fault', and the phrase becomes a refrain. There is no
private system which can be held to account for the tragedy, and
Tony's own concept of order and permanence is rendered useless.
Immediate consolation is provided by the cosmopolitan Mrs Rattery,
who offers Tony a temporary return to the security of childhood, a
game of Animal Snap:

> They were still playing when Albert came in to draw the curtains. Tony had
> only two cards left which he turned over regularly; Mrs Rattery was obliged
> to divide hers, they were too many to hold. They stopped playing when they
> found that Albert was in the room. . . .
> 'We'd better stop.'
> 'It wasn't a very good game. And to think it's the only one you know.'[30]

It is of course the only game that Tony does know, the return to the security and continuity of childhood with its promise of life at Hetton for ever and ever. It is also an ironical comment on Mrs Rattery, for her game is patience:

(Mrs Rattery sat intent over her game, moving little groups of cards adroitly backward and forwards about the table like shuttles across a loom; under her fingers order grew out of chaos; she established sequence and precedence; the symbols before her became coherent, interrelated). . . .

Mrs Rattery brooded over her chequer of cards and then drew them towards her into a heap, haphazard once more and without meaning; it had nearly come to a solution that time, but for a six of diamonds out of place, and a stubbornly congested patch at one corner, where nothing could be made to move. 'It's a heart-breaking game,' she said.[31]

The language is deliberately, mockingly mysterious. Mrs Rattery is after all only playing cards. Yet her adjective 'heartbreaking' is not just fashionable exaggeration, for something much more than the need to conquer boredom is invested in the game.

By his son's death, Tony is thrust into a world 'bereft of order', and in his final recognition of Brenda's duplicity, and the falseness of his belief in her, 'a whole Gothic world had come to grief'; 'there was now no armour glittering through the forest glades, no embroidered feet on the green sward; the cream and dappled unicorns had fled'.[32] Everything upon which Tony had based his existence has been as unreal as the unicorns, yet in reaction against his loss, and in search of renewed purpose and significance, he embarks upon a bizarre version of the romantic quest, a search for the City. Though the City is rumoured to exist in the jungles of Brazil, in Tony's imagination it bears a striking resemblance to Hetton:

His mind was occupied with the City. . . . He had a clear picture of it in his mind. It was Gothic in character, all vanes and pinnacles, gargoyles, battlements, groining and tracery, pavillions and terraces, a transfigured Hetton, pennons and banners floating on the sweet breeze, everything luminous and translucent; a coral citadel crowning a green hill top sewn with daisies, among groves and streams; a tapestry landscape filled with heraldic and fabulous animals and symmetrical, disproportionate blossom.[33]

Tony's quest is a regressive one, a journey not only into the past, but into a mythical past that has never existed. His quest is for something in which he can place his faith, but the outcome of his journey is a complete denial of any such object: 'I will tell you', he declares, 'what I have learned in the forest, where time is different. There is no City. Mrs Beaver has covered it with chromium plating and converted it into flats.'[34] Tony accepts the impossibility of any individual attempt to resist the modern process of standardization. His vision is absurd, a tasteless recreation of vanished glories, indulgent, adolescent romanticism, and yet it is only partly mocked. It is a vision of sorts, an admission of the need to believe in something, and that places it above Mrs Beaver's chromium plating.

For Waugh, the individual's attempt to discover some temporal justification of his own significance is as illusory as Tony's search for the city. No justification exists. The final destination of the search is absurdity. Reading Dickens to a madman in the jungles of Brazil, for ever and ever, Tony has reached his destination. No relationship between individual and reality is possible, because reality as Tony knows it no longer exists. In the story 'Out of Depth', the hero is able to cope with a fundamental change in the nature of reality because of his Catholicism, which is applicable to all realities. Tony, who is quite without significant religious faith, is thereby without the power to cope with change. The mechanistic, modern society cannot be defined by rational means, because it is fundamentally irrational. In Waugh's comic universe, nothing is what it seems. When Tony gives in to the awful Winnie's pleas to be allowed to bathe, he is condemned by those who have overheard, imposing their own interpretations on the incident:

> 'This little girl would like to bathe,' said Tony.
> 'No bathing for children today,' said the beach attendant.
> 'The very idea,' said various onlookers. 'Does he want to drown the child?' 'He's no business to be trusted with children.' '*Unnatural beast.*'
> 'But I *want* to bathe,' said Winnie. 'You said I could bathe if you had two breakfasts.'
> The people who had clustered round to witness Tony's discomfort, looked at one another askance. 'Two breakfasts? Wanting to let the child bathe? The man's balmy.'
> 'Never mind,' said Tony. 'We'll go on the pier.'
> Several of the crowd followed them round the slots, curious to see what new enormity this mad father might attempt. 'There's a man who's eaten two breakfasts and tries to drown his little girl,' they informed other spectators, sceptically observing his attempts to amuse Winnie with skee-ball. Tony's conduct confirmed the view of human nature derived from the weekly newspapers which they had all been reading that morning.[35]

Moral judgements are made arbitrarily – action is subject to any interpretation. Effective communication is impossible because the individual utterance can be referred only to the speaker's own private understanding of the world. There is no shared belief, no common view to which all communication can be ultimately referred. The listener reconstructs what he hears according to his own system, so that for every utterance there are at least two possible interpretations. Each individual understands his relationship to society according to personal priorities. For Tony, they are Hetton and Brenda; for Brenda, a sentimental notion of emancipation. But there are no immutable laws governing human action – only chance; 'Fortune, a much maligned lady'. The plots of Waugh's novels also seem dictated by chance. Events simply occur out of the blue, often literally; Mrs Rattery arrives and departs by aeroplane, and Mr Baldwin drops into the action of *Scoop* by parachute. Incidents are generated by the accidents of circumstance, and like John's death in *A Handful of Dust*, cannot be predicted beforehand nor explained afterwards.

The journeys undertaken through unpredictable worlds by Paul Pennyfeather, Basil Seal, and Tony Last, conform to a basic picaresque pattern. The innocent hero confronts a corrupt and baffling society, and the resulting conflict is the source of comedy. These picaresque journeys – Basil Seal's to Africa, Tony Last's to Brazil, and Paul Pennyfeather's through an equally 'foreign' territory – are quests for knowledge and personal fulfilment; they lead, however, to increasing incomprehension and isolation. The hero is initially forced, by the accidents of circumstance, to abandon his small, comprehensible world, and to face its falseness and its limitations. Yet the new world into which he is thrust turns out to be equally false; the foreign territory is never as it seems, and the conventional morality that the hero carries with him, his gentlemanly code of conduct and evaluation, is quite useless. Paul Pennyfeather is defeated by Margot, Basil Seal by the Emperor Seth, and Tony Last by Mr Todd, simply because these characters act by rules incomprehensible to the innocent hero. Paul Pennyfeather and Basil Seal are allowed to retire in defeat to the small comforts their own comprehensible worlds can offer them, but Tony Last is denied even this consolation.

Evelyn Waugh shared the preoccupations of his contemporaries with social order and individual significance. What distinguishes his thirties fiction is his willingness to consider the forces ranged against him. By and large, he resists the temptation to impose a rather simple notion of belief upon a complex and chaotic reality. Whereas Warner in *The Wild Goose Chase*, Greene in *Brighton Rock*, simplify and sentimentalize reality in deference to their beliefs, Waugh recognizes in his thirties novels that too much may have to be sacrificed for the sake of definitiveness. The attempt at definitiveness does come however, albeit in retrospect. In *Brideshead Revisited*, he returns to the pagan world of 1928–1939', and discerns there 'the divine purpose'.³⁶ Sebastian Flyte and Charles Ryder are both men of the thirties generation, obsessed with its lack of purpose; Charles remembers 'Sebastian looking up at the Colleone statue and saying, "It's rather sad to think that whatever happens you and I can never possibly get involved in a war."'³⁷ Sebastian is dynamic, and Charles is static, and they complement each other in the manner of Peter Beste-Chetwynde and Paul Pennyfeather. Paul and Charles are observers, the sons of convention who are by accident brought into contact with the dynamic world of the Beste-Chetwyndes and the Marchmains. Sebastian's career confirms the implications of Peter's fate at the end of *Decline and Fall* – he becomes a drunkard, his aristocratic beauty and charm no protection against the world. The difference is of course that Sebastian is a Catholic, and by Catholicism his drunkenness and degeneracy are redefined. What is conventionally regarded by Charles as a wasted life, is described by Cordelia as one of beauty and devotion and 'holiness'. Catholicism has in Waugh's eyes the power to change the individual perception of the world; it is an immutable system of values by which action may be judged and evaluated. It is able also to accommodate and justify the anarchic streak that coexisted with his more conventional conservatism; Sebastian Flyte, whom such conservatism would characterize as a bohemian and a wastrel, is classed anew as almost a saint. In *Brideshead Revisited*, Waugh's instinctive sympathy for the reprobate, the character who is outside the rules of society, is sanctioned by Catholicism. When Sebastian declares that 'God prefers drunkards to a lot of respectable people',³⁸ he awards to himself the dignity and significance that Peter Beste-Chetwynde lacks in *Decline and Fall*.

Ryder, to some extent an elaboration of Paul Pennyfeather, is not trapped irrevocably in his 'static' category but offered the possibility of religious belief. This alters his perceptions; chaos becomes order, futility becomes purpose, and he is able to re-define the past by his conversion to Catholicism. The relationship of individual to Catholicism is thus akin to the relationship of individual to revolutionary socialism in *Journey to the Border*. Belief reverses the trend towards chaos. The major difference between Waugh's notion of belief and Upward's, is that Waugh's Catholicism is directed entirely towards re-defining the past. 'My theme', says the narrator, 'is memory'.³⁹ Upward's belief is more concerned with the future, and the conscious awareness that all future action will be undertaken not in isolation but as part of the revolutionary struggle. The fundamental similarity, however, remains; belief re-defines action and existence, making the insignificant significant.

Brideshead Revisited is a surrender to sentimentality. Waugh places the framework of Catholicism over his chaotic thirties universe, and the pieces fit. Yet there is no indication of why they fit. To say that Peter Beste-Chetwynde or Sebastian Flyte is a magical figure with an indefinable sanctity is authorial information, to be taken or left. To say that Catholicism confers that sanctity is an assertion which calls for some kind of verification within the terms of the novel. The order imposed here by Waugh's Catholicism is, like Upward's Marxism, no more logically convincing than any of the other means of ordering existence that are dismissed in *Journey to the Border* or in *A Handful of Dust*. The power of the belief springs not from any inherent compelling logic, but from the individual's overwhelming will to believe. Despite remarks made elsewhere by Waugh concerning the intellectual basis of his belief, Charles Ryder's commitment to Catholicism springs clearly from the need to know that something has come 'out of the fierce little human tragedy in which I played',[40] that he has not, in other words, been merely an actor in a farce. The relationship of individual to Catholicism is thus a reflexive one; the individual believes in God, because Catholicism awards significance to himself and his actions, but it is only capable of doing this because the individual invests Catholicism, by his very will to believe, with the power to do so. This is not to say that Catholicism, once embraced, cannot provide a logical explanation of the significance of all action; merely to say that the attraction of the thirties novelists, Greene and Waugh, towards religion, was not based solely or even mainly on intellectual conviction, but upon the instinctive need for belief. This paradox is at the root of the relationship between the thirties novelists and belief, a cyclical process by which individual and belief are each fundamentally dependent upon the other for significance.

By a chance of literary history, Graham Greene and Evelyn Waugh were both commissioned, quite independently, to visit Mexico in the late thirties, to report on its socialist revolution, and in particular on the oppression of the Catholic Church. Greene spent some two months in the spring of 1938 travelling down by road from Texas to Mexico City, and so on to some of the more remote and little visited parts of Southern Mexico. Waugh followed in the summer of the same year, travelling by his own admission over the beaten tourist tracks, avoiding for the most part the bed-bugs, the dysentery and the squalor that contributed to Greene's hatred of the country.

For both writers, Mexico became what Spain had been for the writers of revolutionary sympathies, a testing ground for the survival of their chosen belief. The experience prompted a reconsideration and affirmation of the function of Catholicism. Mexico was a stage on which the two rival philosophies of the thirties, Catholicism and revolutionary socialism, gave their last performance before more urgent events in Europe distracted the audience's attention. Greene saw in Mexico the final proof of the failure of revolutionary socialism to live up to individual expectations: 'The supporters of the proletarian revolution have staked their lives on a philosophy. It is the only reason they have for going on with the grim job of living. You cannot expect them to admit even to themselves that Russia has proved them wrong – or Mexico – without the comfort of a dramatic conversion to some other faith.'[41] The object of faith is, in Greene's terms, to offer 'comfort'. The comfort to be derived from any 'philosophy' of revolution depended for Greene upon the efficacy of revolutionary action – in Mexico he found abundant evidence of its failure. The philosophy of religion, by implication, does not depend on the quality of human action for its authority and conviction. No matter how corrupt the actions of religious adherents, the power of Catholicism to offer spiritual comfort to the individual is not impaired. In *The Power and the Glory*, based directly on these experiences of Mexico, Greene offers his most clear-cut assertion of the validity of religious over political belief. The final compulsion of Catholicism is contained in the whisky priest's declaration of love for his worldly and corrupt daughter:

He held her tightly by the wrist and suddenly she stayed still, looking up at him. He said, 'I would give my life, that's nothing, my soul . . . my dear, my dear, try to understand that you are – so important.' That was the difference, he had always known, between his faith and theirs, the political leaders of the people who cared only for things like the state, the republic: this child was more important than a whole continent. He said, 'You must take care of yourself because you are so – necessary.'[42]

Political belief, however much it claims to serve the individual, unavoidably denies, in Greene's view, the *value* of the individual. The satisfaction of religious faith lies in the confidence that one is important in the eyes of God.

Waugh's understanding of the Mexican revolution is similar to Greene's, though uncomplicated by any instinctive sympathy for the aims of the revolutionary – he maintains that the suppression of the Church was the direct result of sheer wickedness. What clearly emerges from an otherwise forgettable book is Waugh's abiding fear of social chaos, the very chaos he sees embodied in the Mexican revolution. The suppression of Catholicism is equivalent in Waugh's mind to the destruction of order:

The Catholic believes that in logic and in historical evidence he has grounds for accepting the Church as a society of divine institution, holding a unique commission for her work, privileged on occasions by special revelation glorified continually by members of supernatural sanctity; he finds in her doctrine a philosophy which explains his own peculiar position in the order of the universe, a way of life which makes the earth habitable during his existence there and, after that, according to his merits, the hope of Heaven or the fear of Hell.[43]

Catholicism, then, 'explains' the world, and makes it 'habitable'. Despite differing political sympathies, both Greene and Waugh regarded revolutionary socialism as embodying the threat of uniformity and barbarism that they determined to resist. Conversion to Catholicism was equivalent to a declaration of resistance, a declaration that, contrary to appearance, the modern individual has a significant existence in a significant world.

NOTES

1. *Diaries* p. 237.
2. *A Little Learning* (1964) Chapter Six.
3. 'The Religion of Evelyn Waugh' *Evelyn Waugh and His World* ed Pryce-Jones (1973) pp. 61–2.
4. *Evelyn Waugh* (1975) p. 33.
5. *Diaries* p. 147.
6. Ibid.
7. Ibid pp. 250–1.
8. 'Matter-of-Fact Mothers of the New Age' p. 7.
9. *Labels* (1930) p. 8.
10. 'Out of Depth' (1933) *Mr Loveday's Little Outing and Other Sad Stories* (1936) pp. 136–7.
11. Unsigned 'New Books' *Tablet* 161 (7.1.33) p. 10.
12. D'Arcy et al, 'Mr Evelyn Waugh' *Tablet* 161 (21.1.33) p. 85.
13. Unsigned 'A Recent Novel' *Tablet* 161 (18.2.33) p. 215. A fuller account of the episode is given in F. J. Stopp, *Evelyn Waugh* (1958) pp. 31–2.
14. An Open Letter to H. E. the Cardinal Archbishop of Westminster' (May 1933) p. 1. Unpublished manuscript, held by the Humanities Research Centre in the University of Texas at Austin.
15. Ibid p. 3.
16. 'Fan-Fare' p. 60.
17. *Evelyn Waugh* p. 2.
18. Nancy Cunard et al (eds) *Authors Take Sides on the Spanish War* (1937) no pagination.
19. *Diaries* p. 407.

20. *Robbery Under Law* (1939) pp. 278–9.
21. *Remote People* (1931) p. 180.
22. *Decline and Fall* (1928) p. 162.
23. Ibid p. 248.
24. *Brideshead Revisited* (1945) p. 80.
25. *Decline and Fall* p. 286.
26. *Vile Bodies* (1930) p. 41.
27. Ibid p. 132.
28. Ibid p. 143.
29. Ibid p. 248.
30. *A Handful of Dust* pp. 177–8.
31. Ibid pp. 173–5.
32. Ibid pp. 236–7.
33. Ibid pp. 252–3.
34. Ibid p. 325.
35. Ibid pp. 225–6.
36. 'Warning'. *Brideshead Revisited*. Printed on the dustjacket.
37. *Brideshead Revisited* p. 90.
38. Ibid p. 128.
39. Ibid p. 197.
40. Ibid p. 304.
41. *The Lawless Roads* pp. 271–2.
42. *The Power and the Glory* (1940) p. 102.
43. *Robbery Under Law* pp. 207–8.

Chapter 6

Christopher Isherwood

The novelists so far considered may all be described as committed, but their concerns and the influences upon them were not the exclusive preserve of committed novelists. The effects of upbringing and education; the consciousness of belonging to a unique generation, caught *entre deux guerres*; the consequent attractions of belief – are all characteristic of the middle class, thirties generation of novelists, and not just of those who took the final step of commitment to Marxism or Catholicism. Christopher Isherwood, for example, did neither, but he remains a novelist whose concerns are those of his generation, for whom the relationship of hero and society, individual and belief, are of paramount importance. Isherwood as a young writer manifested the contradictions of outlook characteristic of the thirties, and particularly of the Auden group. Portentousness co-existed with whimsy, self-dramatization with self-depreciation, acerbity with mawkishness. John Lehmann records his impression of Isherwood's 'compelling contradiction and complexity', the 'look of impish fun alternating with the tense concentration of the prophet with a message'.[1] Absorbed in the political developments of Europe, and following them with anxiety, Isherwood seemed at the same time to take an almost masochistic delight in contemplating the imminent destruction of Western civilization. He later admitted that he 'liked to play the front-line alarmist',[2] but this was not equivalent in the eyes of his contemporaries to any fundamental lack of seriousness – it was after all, a characteristic shared by others of the Auden group. Isherwood, in the years before 1939, was regarded by his readers, and to a certain extent by himself, as a left-wing novelist, despite the absence of any real evidence to this effect in his published work. His early novels, *All the Conspirators* (1928) and *The Memorial* (1932), denounce the values of the older generation; the Berlin novels warn of the dangers of Fascism. But they are political only in the most general sense of the word.

Isherwood's fiction of the thirties in fact reveals his profound ambivalence towards the whole question of belief. It is something which he has returned to consider in *Christopher and His Kind*. He was, he recalls, attracted to Communism as a potentially satisfying belief that offered hope for the future; he 'found no difficulty in responding to Communism romantically, as the brotherhood of man'.[3] His admission of romantic response to the 'brotherhood of man' is to some extent tongue-in-cheek, offered as it is in the context of a frank discussion of his homosexuality. At the same time, Isherwood is not denying altogether the essential truth of his statement. The notion of Marxism, as explained to him by Upward, was one in which the forces of history were at work everywhere, 'even in the dullest, stuffiest, most reactionary of settings'. He saw in Upward's Marxism the prospect of transforming the oppressiveness of middle-class England – an oppressiveness which he sought to escape in Berlin – by allying himself with the revolution. He was excited by the possibilities of such a belief. He recalls at the same time his irrepressible doubts, quoting the conclusion of Upward's 'Sunday', in which the hero seeks out the small cell behind the Geisha cafe:

'At first he may be regarded with suspicion, even taken for a police spy. And quite naturally. He will have to prove himself, to prove that he isn't a mere neurotic, an untrustworthy freak. It will take time. But it is the only hope. He will at least have made a start.'

Christopher was thrilled by the austerity of Edward's tone. He was also chilled – more so than he would admit to himself. Did he already know that he would never take the street to that cafe?[4]

Communism offered vitality and purpose, to which Isherwood responded out of the susceptibilities of a generation; but as expressed by Upward, it also suggested a rigid orthodoxy as uncongenial to Isherwood as the repressive values of his elders and his class. In 'Sunday' he seems to have seen the threat to individuality implicit in Upward's concluding sentences, and drawn back. There is no doubt that Isherwood regarded himself, with a mixture of pride and shame, as the 'mere neurotic' and 'untrustworthy freak' for which Upward's revolution had no room. He remained for most of the thirties half way between belief and scepticism, attracted to the one but unable entirely to overcome the other; 'he was what Party dialectiticians used, in those days, to call "unclear"'.[5]

He speaks, in *Christopher and His Kind*, rather patronizingly of his 'romantic' attraction to Communism, and he could, even in the thirties, expose the sentimentality of any desire for the 'meaning of existence': 'In another moment, when I had drunk exactly the right amount of champagne, I should have a vision. I took a sip. And now, with extreme clarity, without passion or malice, I saw what Life really is. It had something, I remember, to do with the revolving sunshade.'[6] This scene in *Mr Norris Changes Trains* is echoed in *Goodbye to Berlin* when Christopher returns to a dive he used to frequent with his friend Fritz: 'It was all just as we had left it; only less sinister, less picturesque, symbolic no longer of a tremendous truth about the meaning of existence – because, this time, I wasn't in the least drunk.'[7] In both instances, the meaning of life is described as a drunken illusion, the language deliberately echoing both the pomposity and the temerity of those who seek, and claim to have found, blanket solutions to the problem of living. Yet in each case the narrator is not parodying others, but himself, and his own weakness for such solutions. He is in sympathy with the desire for 'meaning', but, like Waugh in *A Handful of Dust*, is also able to mock the attendant risks of sentimentality and over-simplification.

Isherwood's narrator in *Goodbye to Berlin* is essentially a detached observer, but the consolations of detachment often seem to be meagre. He is a man of the thirties, an observer of contemporary society who is also aware that he is implicated in its fate. When Fraulein Schroeder begins her favourite monologue about her lodgers of the past, Herr Issyvoo does not catch her mood of nostalgia; it prompts in him quite a different reaction, a compelling statement of the thirties generation's dread of insignificance and futility:

When I have been listening to her for some time, I find myself relapsing into a curious trance-like state of depression. I begin to feel profoundly unhappy. Where are all those lodgers now? Where, in another ten years, shall I be myself? Certainly not here. How many seas and frontiers shall I have to cross to reach that distant day; how far shall I have to travel, on foot, on horseback, by car, push-bike, aeroplane, steamer, train, lift, moving-staircase and tram? How much money shall I need for that enormous journey? How much food must I gradually, wearily consume on my way? How many pairs of shoes shall I wear out? How many thousands of cigarettes shall I smoke? How many cups of tea shall I drink and how many glasses of beer? What an awful tasteless prospect![8]

The journey through life that Isherwood's narrator describes is a kind of mirror image of George's journey in *The Wild Goose Chase* – it is a journey without a defining purpose. There is no one frontier or border to be crossed, but an infinity of them, stretching dauntingly into the distance. The passage itself is a vast catalogue of actions, but meaningless actions, without any faith or belief that might render them significant. It makes, particularly in the context of the thirties, for a frightening prospect – that the individual existence is but an accumulation of meaningless actions, to no discernible purpose. The scorn the narrators of the Berlin novels feel for any claim to discover 'the meaning of existence', must then be balanced by 'Christopher's' expression here of the fear that there is no meaning at all.

It is this fear that lies behind the attraction of both narrators towards the Communist Party. In *Mr Norris Changes Trains*, William is deeply moved by his first experience of a Party meeting:

I had never been to a communist meeting before, and what struck me most was the fixed attention of the upturned rows of faces; faces of the Berlin working class, pale and prematurely lined, often haggard and ascetic, like the heads of scholars, with thin, fair hair brushed back from their broad fore-heads. They had not come here to see each other or to be seen, or even to fulfil a social duty. They were attentive, but not passive. They were not spectators. They participated, with a curious, restrained passion, in the speech made by the red-haired man. He spoke for them, he made their thoughts articulate. They were listening to their own collective voice. At intervals they applauded it, with sudden, spontaneous violence. Their passion, their strength of purpose elated me. I stood outside it. One day, perhaps, I should be with it, but never of it.[9]

Samuel Hynes in his book *The Auden Generation* sees this as an expression of genuine regret, a characteristic reaction of the young middle-class Englishman who regards himself as unworthy and un-qualified to fight on the side of revolution.[10] The attitude certainly was not unusual; Geoffrey Gorer, for example, blamed his failure to join the Party on his own 'cowardice and laziness', and castigated himself for lacking 'the unbelievable cool courage of the ardent communist'.[11] This kind of self-delusion is not however William's – he admits that his feelings are 'muddled', but not that he feels inferior to the mass of communists assembled to hear Mr Norris speak. His statement that 'one day, perhaps, I shall be with it, but never of it', is a clear recognition that he can never belong to this group and share its purpose, but it is also an assertion of determination, not to sacrifice his individuality to a 'collective voice'. William is distinct from the mass, and he means to maintain that distinction. It is the same value placed upon individuality that prevented Isherwood taking 'the street to that cafe'. William's description of the meeting contains both the attractions and the dangers of commitment; the individual pur-pose that undoubtedly springs from a collective cause is outweighed by the paradoxical suppression of individuality that the cause de-mands of its adherents. In 'The Nowaks' section of *Goodbye to Berlin*, Otto announces to his family that Christopher is a Communist. 'Not a proper one, I'm afraid,'[12] replies Christopher importantly. But in the last 'Berlin Diary', he is asked by a young member of a Communist pathfinder group whether he is a communist, and the answer is 'no':

I asked if there were any girls in his pathfinder group. Rudi was as shocked as if I'd said something really indecent.

'Women are no good,' he told me bitterly. 'They spoil everything. They haven't got the spirit of adventure. Men understand each other much better when they're alone together. Uncle Peter (that's our Scoutmaster) says women should stay at home and mend socks. That's all they're fit for!'

'Is Uncle Peter a Communist, too?'

'Of course!' Rudi looked at me suspiciously. 'Why do you ask that?'

'Oh, no special reason,' I replied hastily. 'I think perhaps I was mixing him up with somebody else. . . .'[13]

The implied equation with Nazism is not a simple one. Christopher remains sympathetic to Communism, and antipathetic to Nazism, but the regimentation and narrow-mindedness of the pathfinder group is not for him.

In *The Wild Goose Chase* and *Journey to the Border*, Rex Warner and Edward Upward both came up against the fundamental contradictoriness of their understanding of Marxism. It was a belief which satisfactorily explained the world and the individual's function within it, and brought accordingly a sense of purpose to the individual; at the same time, the very nature of revolutionary action demanded a conscious abnegation of the rights of individuality in the interests of the cause. It was a problem that Rex Warner in particular returned to repeatedly in the thirties. Isherwood recognized the same paradox, not as an artistic problem to be overcome but as the very subject of his fiction – both *Mr Norris Changes Trains* and *Goodbye to Berlin* consider the inherent conflict between the desire for belief and the desire for self-assertion.

In the terminology of Isherwood's school and undergraduate days, it was necessary to pass the 'Test', that mysterious hurdle placed in front of 'the truly weak man'. Failure meant submission to the oppressive power of society, success meant entry to that elite who had answered society's demands. In the metaphor of the test, the young Isherwood revealed his desire for the approbation of society. But in the early novels, society itself, and the rules by which it 'tests' the individual, is rejected as stultifying. Isherwood became increasingly conscious during the thirties of the implication of his youthful formulation – one passed 'the test' by conforming. In *All the Conspirators* and *The Memorial* Isherwood's heroes are more concerned to escape altogether the rules and constrictions of their bourgeois upbringing, and to discover approbation elsewhere. The central relationship of *All the Conspirators* is that between the hero and his mother. Mrs Lindsay's strong maternal hold upon Philip is also the hold of her generation's values, and he longs to escape. Philip's desire for self-assertion focusses upon a notion of himself as an artist – as one who by his creative genius will place himself outside the bounds of convention, into the free realm of art. His submission to rheumatic fever, and to the devoted care of his mother, is a renunciation of his claims as an artist, and thereby of his rights to individuality. He accepts limitations upon himself in return for the consolation and security of his mother's comprehensible world. Philip is a thirties hero, unsure of himself and of his power to resist the constricting force of his society. Against him Isherwood poses the character of Allen Chalmers (based upon Edward Upward), an heroic but vaguely defined figure who has resisted the very forces to which Philip succumbs, retaining his integrity and right to self-determination. The relationship between these two characters is one between two potential heroes – the sensitive young man who lacks the strength and moral courage to survive unaided outside the world he despises, and the 'truly strong man' who draws his strength and his individuality from an unexplained source.

The Memorial elaborates upon this relationship, between the nominal hero and a kind of alternative hero, but here the relationship is by no means so clear-cut. Eric Vernon resembles in many ways Philip Lindsay; he is uncertain, caught in an oppressive relationship with a mother who is concerned only with the past, the 'old, safe, beautiful world'. His cousin Maurice, like Chalmers in *All the Conspirators*, seems, by his looks and his charm and his confidence, to lie outside the dictates of conventional society, answerable to some other law. Eric looks upon Maurice as Paul Pennyfeather does upon Peter Beste-Chetwynde – with the envy and admiration that the 'static' character feels for the 'dynamic'. Like Waugh, Isherwood poses this notion of a spiritual aristocracy only to question its basis. Eric recognizes that Maurice, despite his great charm and his air of unaccountability, is directionless and self-destructive. In *All the Conspirators*, he has suggested through Allen Chalmers the possibility of resisting the oppressive power of society simply by one's confidence to do so; he pursues the notion in *The Memorial*, to suggest through Maurice that such self-confidence is completely vulnerable. Eric Vernon is unlike Philip Lindsay in that he does not return to his mother and the regressive values she represents. He does recognize, like Philip, that he cannot free himself from the past by a simple act of will, but there *are* other possibilities. Belief offers the justification of individual existence that the hero requires. The process of self-assertion thus becomes a part of the process of commitment to some kind of belief, and Eric is faced with the familiar choice. The possibilities of social action seem too remote, too inaccessible to someone of his class and background. Instead we learn at the end of the novel of Eric's conversion to Catholicism – the thirties hero has presumably found what he is after.

It is difficult to know quite how seriously to take this final commitment to Catholicism, coming as it does after Eric's earlier interest in Communism. It may well be an admission of defeat, that Catholicism, to which Isherwood claims to have felt no personal attraction, did indeed offer the only available solution to the predicament of the thirties hero. Isherwood recalls that in 1938 he was set firmly against the consolations of religion, and indeed of any kind of belief, doubting 'if one ever accepts a belief until one urgently needs it. But, although Christopher wasn't yet aware that he needed such a belief, he may have been feeling the need subconsciously. This would explain his recently increased hostility towards what he thought of as "religion" – the version of Christianity he had been taught in his childhood. Perhaps he was afraid that he would be forced to accept it, at last, after nearly fifteen years of atheism.'[14] On the evidence of the thirties novels, this awareness of the need for belief was less subconscious than Isherwood remembers. In any event, the 'religion' referred to here, middle-class Anglicanism, is more closely related to the bourgeois values that Eric rejects than to the Catholicism he embraces. In *The Memorial*, Catholicism is presented as something quite different; it is, with Communism, a radical alternative to the *status quo*, offering the individual the required means of comprehending his environment and fulfilling his individual potential. What emerges clearly from *The Memorial* is the importance of the need for faith. True to the times, the possibilities are presented as Catholicism and Communism, but neither possibility is explored with any rigour. The emphasis is not upon the object of faith but upon the hero's despair, his rejection of the values of his parents' generation, and his consequent receptivity to some kind – one might almost say any kind – of belief.

All the Conspirators and *The Memorial* are intensely partisan statements of the problems facing the thirties generation. They deal with the search by the young middle-class hero for alternatives to the world of manners and convention. The opposition in both novels is clear, and open to little modification – youth versus age. This opposition is paralleled on a formal level by the use of conventional and experimental methods. Under the influence of Joyce in particular,

Isherwood used the interior monologue freely in *All the Conspirators*, but as he himself pointed out, only with the younger characters: 'Mrs Lindsay is never allowed to think in this way, however; neither is Miss Durrant or Colonel Page or Mr Langbridge. What kind of chauvinism is at work here? Victor is on the side of the enemy in this story while Miss Durrant is at worst a very benevolent neutral. Ah yes – but Victor is under twenty-five, while poor Miss Durrant is over forty!'[15] The opposition becomes so rigid in the novel that it even overrules its own exceptions – characters who are not directly condemned for belonging to the older generation are just as effectively dismissed by their inability to speak through interior monologue. Isherwood saw the unconscious rigidity of his use of this method as symptomatic of a wider misunderstanding of the nature of literary innovation:

I can excuse the echoes of E. M. Forster and Virginia Woolf [in *All the Conspirators*], because the author has actually learned a few lessons from these masters and put them into practice here. But the echoes of James Joyce annoy me, because they are merely echoes. I find this repeated use of the Joycean thought-stream technique jarringly out of style. Its self-consciously grim, sardonically detached tone doesn't suit any of these characters; even coming from Allen Chalmers it rings false. . . . The narrative trick of jumping almost every important scene and then describing it in jerky flashbacks, now seems to me most tiresome. Here is an example of a valuable lesson learned from Forster which has been reduced to absurdity through over-application.[16]

In his concern to penetrate to the central problems of his hero in particular, he relied greatly on this combination of 'thought-stream' and 'flashback':

Voice from the non-existent past. Ventriloquized through the lips of a pre-post-mid-Edwardian suburban clerk, sneering, with boils.
But I exaggerate. And for a purpose.
She said:
They oughtn't to have. I quite agree. And I shouldn't dream of asking him. If I'd been there I'd have kept you in better order.
Why can't you say frankly that you're shocked, too?
Blushing. A boy's quarrel with his governess.
Well then, I am.
Very much?
Terribly.
Smiling, absent-minded banter. Glancing for just an instant at her wrist.[17]

Isherwood was the first of his contemporaries to abandon this method – not only was it derivative, but it seemed to be heading in quite a different direction from his major concerns, away from the relationship of individual to society, and towards preciousness.

In this retrospective criticism of his early work, Isherwood speaks respectfully of 'these masters', Forster and Woolf. His admiration was double-edged, particularly in the case of Virginia Woolf, but it does indicate that the left-wing writers of the thirties, and the Auden group in particular, did not institute a simple reaction against Bloomsbury and the twenties. Stephen Spender, in his autobiography, would seem to suggest that the thirties were utterly new: 'To them [Bloomsbury] there was something barbarous about our generation. It seemed that with us the thin wall which surrounded their little situation of independence and which enabled them to retain their air of being the last of the Romans had broken down. A new generation had arisen which proclaimed that bourgeois civilization was at an end, and which assumed the certainty of revolution, which took sides and which was exposed even within its art to the flooding-in of public events, which cared but little for style and knew nothing of Paris.'[18] This may be true to what Spender saw as the spirit of the thirties but it cannot be taken too literally. The thirties reaction against insularity did not exclude an often sentimental faith in the importance of the individual relationships, even when, as in the fiction of the thirties generation, such relationships generally proved unsatisfying of themselves. Spender, in chastising Bloomsbury, chooses to ignore the similarities of the two generations in order to emphasize the dramatic break between futility and purpose. Isherwood became gradually aware that the two generations could not be so easily categorized, with moral judgements made on the basis of birthdays.

Christopher Isherwood was the most receptive of his generation to the work of his immediate predecessors. His regard for Forster and Woolf centred on what he saw as their ability to 'tea-table' it; to write of fundamental issues in unsensational prose. For Isherwood, Forster was a 'comic writer', and 'that was our great slogan, Edward Upward's and mine, when we were young, that we were going to be essentially comic writers, since tragedy was no longer modern'.[19] This last phrase, itself both portentous and flip, serious and comic, goes to the core of the problem faced by this generation of novelists. They had serious things to say, but seriousness is close to earnestness, a trap that none of them entirely avoided. It may well be too that to be profoundly serious without also being either pompous or banal demands a rare level of genius. Certainly any attempt to confront the problems of the times and to offer solutions, in *The Wild Goose Chase*, in *Journey to the Border*, in *Brighton Rock, Brideshead Revisited*, or *The Memorial*, led to sentimentality and over-simplification. It is only when these novelists allow their prose to explore rather than dictate, when the authorial perspective is detached rather than involved, that seriousness survives intact below the surface. The slogan 'tragedy was no longer modern' belonged to both Upward and Isherwood, but only Isherwood was able to put its implications into effect. In the Berlin novels, he moves towards understatement, by which the large issues, of self-determination, of the individual's relationship to his society, of the function of belief, are not confronted head-on but approached obliquely through Isherwood's famous camera-eye. The camera photographs the surface, and what lies beneath the surface is only implied.

Isherwood records how in the late twenties he developed 'a superstitious faith in the power of exact reporting'.[20] The term 'reportage' to describe this kind of obsessive naturalism gained currency in the thirties, and became increasingly allied with the Left. It was primarily a term which codified the sense of reaction many left-wing writers of the thirties felt against the twenties; it asserted the importance of the real world over the introspective individual. Reportage was not however merely a reaction against the decadence of formal experiment – it appealed also as a political tool. The editor of *Left Review* in 1935, Montagu Slater, affirmed the potential power of 'descriptive reporting', seeing it as 'something which the tabloid press has almost replaced by wisecracks, which the revolutionary press has often no room for, and which for one reason and another has a particularly revolutionary import. (We have even invented a jargon name for it, "reportage".) Certainly to describe things as they are is a revolutionary act in itself. . . . It can also be one of the most effective means of changing an enemy's mind.'[21] This belief, that clear-eyed description of 'things as they are' could sway the reader politically, was the basis for considering the proletarian novel as revolutionary, even when the content seemed to be pointing in another direction, towards cynicism and resignation. The hopes placed by many people in 'reportage' sprang from the desire to close the gap between art and life, and seemed for many the solution to the problem which plagued left-wing writers of the thirties, the problem of achieving social and political relevance. It meant in effect a movement away from authorial didacticism towards a kind of impersonal didacticism which would spring from the very subject of the text. By the removal of personal bias, the subject-matter would be seen more clearly to refer to every individual, and every individual would feel himself implicated in the described reality.

The importance of impersonal description received a certain scientific cachet with the establishment in the late thirties of the sociological movement, Mass Observation. The poet and sociologist Charles Madge put forward his ideas for a collective record of British contemporary life in all its mundane aspects in an article for *Left Review* in February of 1937, in which he outlined the function of the 'artist-scientist'. 'His problem is not to raise to the level of his own consciousness aspects of humanity hitherto concealed or only guessed at, but he has to raise the level of consciousness collectively of the whole mass, he has to induce self-realization on a mass scale. He becomes, that is to say, the organizer of collective human-scientific activity, and his poem or thesis becomes a report of this collective achievement.'[22] Madge's assumption is basically akin to that of the supporters of 'reportage' – the function of the artist, the impersonal observer, is to induce by his faithful record of conditions, 'self-realization on a mass-scale'. This is in itself a political act, for the other half of this kind of self-realization is revolutionary action. Madge's statement of intent contains a fundamental implication for the revolutionary artist, one which both Edward Upward and Rex Warner found impossible to accept – it denies the significance of the individual. On the one hand it denies the significance of the individual reader, who is lost in Madge's collective consciousness. On the other, it denies the significance of the individual artist. For Warner and Upward and other writers of the Auden group, the artist had a specific and valuable function – 'reportage' seemed to suggest he was little more than a technician. Madge claims that the function of the artist is 'not to raise to the level of his own consciousness aspects of humanity hitherto concealed or only guessed at'; as far as this can be successfully interpreted, it seems to be stating precisely what Upward and Warner did regard as the function of the novelist – to bring to the surface those aspects of reality which were not immediately apparent, to encourage the reader to go beneath the apparent oppressiveness and discover those fundamental values which would support and console the individual. For many writers of left-wing sympathies, reportage or exact reporting seemed less and less political and more and more merely descriptive. If the function of the artist was indeed to interpret reality rather than present it unadorned, that implied what Spender called 'two approaches to the contemporary political scene: the one is direct, or partially satiric, external presentation; the other is fantasy or allegory'.[23] The split in left-wing writing in the thirties was thus one between 'reportage' and what might be called 'expressionism' – between the proletarian novel, and the novel of revolutionary commitment as practised by Upward and Warner.

Christopher Isherwood fits into neither category. His novel-world is clearly a realistic one, and not the expressionist or allegorical world of Upward or of Warner. Yet it cannot be classed as 'reportage'. While his novel-world is 'real', it is also subject to artistic manipulation. Of course, to distinguish Isherwood's prose from the general category of 'reportage' is strictly speaking artificial, simply because the term 'reportage' is itself an artificial one. All descriptive writing, no matter how detached or impersonal, is subject to selection and manipulation of some kind. Madge's 'artist-scientist', who acts as a kind of amanuensis for the spirit of exact reporting, is simply an impossibility. The difference between Isherwood and the 'Mass Observers' is therefore largely one of degree, between those who favour, to use Isherwood's own term against him, 'the power of exact reporting', and those who, like Isherwood himself, favour the power of the artist to place, select, and comment upon the fruits of his observations.

The narrators of the Berlin novels maintain a protective detachment from the world they observe. The society in which they move, Berlin of the early thirties, is a volatile one, with potential chaos only just below the surface. William Bradshaw and 'Christopher Isherwood' avoid the implications of this potential chaos by taking the superficial view. The world which the narrator only half-inhabits seems constantly to be threatening to draw him in, compromising his detachment and overwhelming his precarious individuality and separateness. As Christopher and Otto are leaving the sanatorium after having visited Frau Nowak, Christopher feels obscurely threatened by the patients who crowd round the bus to say goodbye:

> They all thronged round us for a moment in the little circle of light from the panting bus, their lit faces ghastly like ghosts against the black stems of the pines. This was the climax of my dream: the instant of nightmare in which it would end. I had an absurd pang of fear that they were going to attack us – a gang of terrifyingly soft muffled shapes – clawing us from our seats, dragging us hungrily down, in dead silence. But the moment passed. They drew back – harmless, after all, as mere ghosts – into the darkness, while our bus, with a great churning of its wheels, lurched forward towards the city, through the deep unseen snow.[24]

It is Christopher's nightmare, that the army of ghosts will surround him, claiming his youth and vitality for their own. He must continue his journey, though the road ahead remains 'unseen'. It is not a journey towards anything definable, but a journey away from the threat to his individuality and his very existence posed by these tubercular ghosts. The climax of the narrator's bad dream lies in his submission to his surroundings, his abandonment of individuality.

Isherwood's narrators preserve their independence, and the complacent simplicity of their world view, by an apparently impenetrable naivety. When William Bradshaw first meets Arthur Norris in a train returning to Berlin, he cannot help but notice that his travelling companion is acutely agitated over the imminent Customs inspection at the German border. William, however, arrives at 'a satisfactory explanation of his behaviour. . . . The old boy was engaged in a little innocent private smuggling. Probably a piece of silk for his wife or a box of cigars for a friend. And now, of course, he was beginning to feel scared. Certainly he looked prosperous enough to pay any amount of duty. The rich have strange pleasures'.[25] Confident of his own sophistication, the narrator is able patronizingly to dismiss Mr Norris' supposedly petty cares, and to arrive at a smug homily. As the novel progresses, it becomes clear that this summing-up of Mr Norris has been superficial and wrong. William too easily accepts the apparent explanation as the only explanation of action and events, and does not admit the possibility of other more complex, and less acceptable motivations. The older William, looking back, continually mocks the naivety of his youthful self. At Olga's brothel, William is shocked to hear his new friend screaming piteously from another room, where as the reader has already guessed, Arthur's sexual preferences are being gratified: 'There was no mistaking the voice. They had got Arthur in there, and were robbing him and knocking him about. I might have known it. We were fools ever to have poked our noses into a place like this.'[26] The older, more sophisticated William who is writing the novel is understandably amused at his mistake. The implication is, now that William has become a man of experience, he realizes how simple had been his earlier impressions of Mr Norris. He seems even to realize the dangers in drawing firm conclusions from superficial understanding. The process is however more complicated:

I was fond of Arthur with an affection strengthened by obstinacy. If my friends didn't like him because of his mouth or his past, the loss was theirs; I was, I flattered myself, more profound, more human, an altogether subtler connoisseur of human nature than they. And if, in my letters to England, I sometimes referred to him as 'a most amazing old crook,' I only meant by this that I wanted to imagine him as a glorified being; audacious and self-reliant, reckless and calm. All of which, in reality, he only too painfully and obviously wasn't.[27]

The narrator deflates his earlier self-importance, but his own conclusion is itself superficial. Behind the two levels of William the narrator is the author, who calls into question the judgements of both the younger and the older William. Isherwood provides us with a wider interpretation of Mr Norris than either William the actor or William the narrator is able to arrive at; the narrator's judgements, even those in which he comments ironically upon his former naivety, are at best one aspect of the truth.

The limitations upon the narrator's understanding are apparent in the episode towards the end of the novel, when Arthur arranges for William to accompany Baron von Pregnitz to a Swiss ski resort, where he is to be contacted by 'Margot', the mysterious sender of telegrams. Arthur gives William a bland and unlikely explanation for the trip, and evades William's suspicious questions: 'As a final test, I tried to look Arthur in the eyes. But no, this time-honoured process didn't work. Here were no windows to the soul. They were merely part of his face, light-blue jellies, like naked shell-fish in the crevices of a rock.'[28] William accepts the conventional rule of appearances – that the eyes will somehow yield up secrets. His conception of Mr Norris as delightfully amoral does not include a Mr Norris who is capable of betraying the Baron to save his own skin. Only afterwards, when he learns of Arthur's cruel manipulation of the unfortunate Baron and his cynical use of William in the plot, does the young man genuinely suspect another side to his friend's character. Even Arthur's much celebrated commitment to the party has been false. This unlooked for revelation spurs William to a final attempt to get to the root of Mr Norris' character, but he lacks the experience, or the necessary sophistication, to disarm such an old master: 'It was no good; we had returned to our verbal card-playing. The moment of frankness, which might have redeemed so much, had been elegantly avoided. . . . Here we were, as so often before, at the edge of that delicate, almost invisible line which divided our two worlds. We should never cross it now.'[29] William retreats from his attempt to understand Mr Norris, and regards him once more as a 'character'.

William bases his conclusions upon a superficial understanding of reality. When he is forced to accept a different notion of reality, he is unable to assimilate it. The solution is to retreat into the consolations of superficiality, and ignore the facts. He consistently falls victim to his belief in the significance of appearances, and his ability to extrapolate correctly from them. Unsure of Margot's identity, he settles upon an appropriately sinister figure, and ignores the harmless looking Dutch businessman who does not conform to his romantic notion of international spy and *agent provocateur*. The sinister figure, himself a novelist, caricatures William's mode of perception; '"I write very quick," he informed us. "For me, one glance is sufficient. I do not believe in the second impression."'[30] William is at least susceptible to the second impression, but he cannot bear too much reality, or too great a strain upon his superficial romanticism. The revelation of Mr Norris's evil and corruption is too much for William, and he retreats from its implications. William reacts instinctively against evil and unpleasantness. He feels an immediate antipathy towards Mr Norris' secretary: 'He had watery light yellow eyes and a blotched complexion the colour of porridge. His head was huge and round, set awkwardly on a short plump body. He wore a smart lounge-suit and patent-leather shoes. I didn't like the look of him at all.'[31] Schmidt is the embodiment of evil, and he is also Mr Norris' other half, his corrupt self who cannot be discarded. At the end of the novel, their partnership is indissoluble; 'they are doomed to walk the Earth together'.[32] The sordid aspects of Mr Norris' character, contained in the repellent Schmidt, are beyond William's ability to comprehend; he is unable to cope with the evil of the world.

For William, Mr Norris remains an enigma. For Isherwood, Mr Norris is a product of both good and evil, of innocence and corruption, and one must come to terms with both elements in order to understand him. Describing Olga, the brothel-madam, William unconsciously states the problem; 'she was a procuress, a cocaine-seller and a receiver of stolen goods; she also let lodgings, took in washing and, when in the mood, did exquisite fancy needlework. Arthur once showed me a table-centre she had given him for Christmas which was quite a work of art.'[33] Olga's divided character defies simple explanation. Isherwood seems to be accepting not only the existence of evil, but its inevitability, as the mirror image of good. One is dependent upon the other. Orwell expressed the relationship in similar terms, when he observed that 'Al Capone was the best of husbands and fathers, and that Joseph Smith (of brides in the bath fame) was sincerely loved by ths first of his seven wives and always returned to her between murders'.[34] Isherwood suggests some kind of resolution of this anomaly in the 'exquisite fancy needlework' that Olga produces. Out of the disparate elements within reality and character comes a work of art, which contains and at the same time is greater than its parts. It is no great step from this to see Isherwood's own work of art, the novel, as containing and preserving all the elements of the world he describes in static harmony, and indeed the narrator of *Goodbye to Berlin* makes this claim specifically on the first page of the novel.

Information in *Goodbye to Berlin* is apparently recorded arbitrarily, but it is made clear from the beginning that the novel does not purport to be an impersonal record of reality – it is an artistic version of it; 'some day, all this will have to be developed, carefully printed, fixed'.[35] The photographic observations which comprise *Goodbye to Berlin* have been developed, printed, selected and arranged in a particular way. Subjective art is created by the manipulation of 'objective' reporting, so that *Goodbye to Berlin* becomes the artist's version of a period and place, no longer transient but 'fixed'. Isherwood has, in the terminology of photography, 'fixed' the images, made them fast. He has also, as a conscious artist, fixed his material by tampering with it, imposing an artistic unity upon an ununified reality. There are three 'Christopher Isherwood's' in *Goodbye to Berlin*. He is first of all the charming innocent whom everyone likes, with whom they feel at ease. He attracts their confessions. Secondly, he is self-aware – aware that he is a 'bit of a sham', that his mannerisms are a means of maintaining distance from those with whom he feels vulnerable – 'smiling sourly, adopting instinctively the armour of sulky eccentricity which protects me on such occasions, I advanced hobbling into their midst'[36] – aware that he is slightly ridiculous, with his 'arty talk to lady pupils' and his 'newly acquired parlour socialism'. But there is a third aspect of the narrator which casts some doubt on the complete veracity of the second. He is a reporter, and his whole *milieu* is raw material. The apparently candid admission of the protective 'armour' is misleading. Armour can also disguise, and it is in this disguise of innocence and slight eccentricity that he can observe, as it were, unobserved.

When Fraulein Schroeder is endeavouring to explain Fraulein Kost's occupation, she performs a coquettish pantomime, 'waddling across the kitchen like a duck, mincingly holding a duster between her finger and thumb. "I don't quite understand, Fraulein Schroeder," says Christopher. "Do you mean that she's a tight-rope walker?"'[37] Christopher's reference several lines later to one of Fraulein Kost's customers makes it clear that he is consciously using his naivety as a device to ingratiate himself by his apparently unconscious humour; the personality he reveals to others is a deliberate creation, protecting his true self. Christopher refrains from committing himself, avoiding the threat to his individuality and self-sufficiency posed by the problems of others. He is attracted to emotional involvement, just as he is attracted to the Communist Party, but he resists both, seeing in them the potential suffocation of his self, the absorption of individuality in something larger than individuals. At the very beginning of *Goodbye to Berlin*, Christopher describes the call that is 'sure to sound, so piercing, so insistent, so despairingly human, that at last I have to get up and peep through the slats of the venetian blind to make quite sure that it is not – as I know very well it could not possibly be – for me'.[38] It is the call that Christopher both longs for and dreads, the call to involvement and self-abnegation which he consistently resists.

Unlike William, Christopher is cynical beneath his naivety. He is aware that in seeking to define action and render it significant, we are also tempted to sentimentalize it. In the same way, political belief, which does seem to codify and justify and explain the superficial reality, also for Isherwood impossibly simplifies it. He recalls in *Journey to a War*, the record of his travels with Auden to China in 1938, an address he gave to three hundred trainee propagandists for the defence against Japanese aggression; 'it is strange to have to talk to an audience which does not understand a single word you are saying. One's natural instinct is to shout at them as though they were deaf, or simply to make horrible faces and wave the arms like a windmill. . . . "You must win this war," I boomed, "to save China, to save Japan, to save Europe"'. Isherwood is both involved in a political cause and at the same time aware of the superficial anomalies which render such a commitment itself superficial; the speech he is delivering so bombastically and urgently is being translated into Chinese: 'It seemed to us that they were making quite a different speech, much longer, all on their own.'[39] To accuse Isherwood here of insensitive whimsy in the face of larger issues is to miss the point. Rather he is acutely aware of the importance of the 'superficial', and its refusal often to conform to a set of rules governed by the deeper forces of historical inevitability. The attractions of belief, the individual's desire to belong, are both central to Isherwood's fiction of the late twenties and the thirties, but at the same time he is aware of the desire to remain apart, to distinguish the self from the mass. Rex Warner, Edward Upward, and other writers of the Auden group, found, for a limited time at least, that literary Marxism satisfied both criteria; they subscribed to a belief that was universally applicable, and by doing so belonged to a group that was exclusive. Isherwood discovered this double sense, of belonging to a group of like-minded while retaining one's sense of difference from the mass, elsewhere, in his homosexuality, and in the philosophy of Vedanta.

Homosexuality embodied his rebellion against everything English and middle-class, and offered instead another kind of society, with its own rules and its own definitions of action:

Girls are what the State and the Church and the Law and the Press and the Medical profession endorse, and command me to desire. My mother endorses them, too. She is silently, brutishly willing me to get married and breed grandchildren for her. Her will is the will of Nearly Everybody, and in their will is my death. *My* will is to live according to my nature, and to find a place where I can be what I am. . . . But I'll admit this – even if my nature were like theirs, I should still have to fight them, in one way or another. If boys didn't exist, I should have to invent them.[40]

With the benefit of hindsight, Isherwood defines what at the time he instinctively felt. His homosexuality constituted a kind of self-assertion by defiance, because only by defying the dominant society and its imposed values could he hang on to his individuality – to submit is, as he describes it, to die. The individual cannot, however, stand alone against society. He requires some support. The camaraderie of homosexuality in the thirties seems to have been for Isherwood a kind of secret brotherhood, an alliance of initiates who, to use a phrase from *Lions and Shadows*, saw through, and stood up to, the 'tremendous and imposing bluff' of conventional society. But continued resistance to the imposition of conformity can be a wearing process, requiring constant defensiveness. It seems in the end a rather cheerless means of establishing individuality. Vedanta offered another way.

Isherwood's interest in Vedanta began in late 1939, and by 1941 he was effectively committed to it as the philosophy by which he would live. His susceptibility to Vedanta came from his rejection of the efficacy of political action, and his accompanying dissatisfaction with scepticism as an alternative: 'By the time Auden and I sailed for the United States I had realized that I was, and perhaps had really always been, a pacifist.'[41] Reflecting the characteristic need of the thirties writer to believe in something, he defines his doubts as the evidence of an unconscious belief in pacifism. But Isherwood regarded pacifism as a negative rather than a positive belief, the embodiment of his rejection of political force:

That was all I had left to go on with [in 1939]: a negation. For, as I now began to realize, my whole political position, left-wing anti-fascist, had been based on the acceptance of armed force. All the slogans I had been repeating and living by were essentially militaristic. Very well: throw them out. But what remained? I told myself that I should have to put my emotions back from a political on to a personal basis. I would be an individual again, with my own values, my own kind of integrity. This sounded challenging and exciting. But it raised a disconcerting question: 'what were the values to be?'[42]

Isherwood declares that his intention at the end of the thirties was to seek his 'own values', but this is followed immediately by the question 'what were these values to be'. He does not mean that he sought to *invent* his own values, but that he sought the elusive and immutable values that would apply to his predicament. What he needed was 'a brand-new vocabulary . . . with a set of philosophical terms which were exact in meaning, unemotive, untainted by disgusting old associations with clergymen's sermons, schoolmasters' pep talks, politicians' patriotic speeches'.[43] What he needed was an entirely new Faith. His instinct, as revealed in all his thirties fiction, was that reality could not be rigidly defined or evaluated according to any one system. It is therefore both ironical and devastatingly logical that he should subscribe to a belief – Vedanta – that maintained just that position.

Vedanta, as Isherwood understood it, questioned his own and by implication the conventional Western understanding of what constitutes individuality. He sums up the difference in his introduction to *Vedanta for the Western World*. 'Every time you desire, or fear, or hate; every time you boast or indulge your vanity; every time you struggle to get something for yourself, you are really asserting: "I am a separate, unique individual, I stand apart from everything else in the universe." But you don't, you know.'[44] The essential self only emerges when the individual accepts that he is part of all creation, not when he continues to maintain his separateness from it. Whereas the narrators of the Berlin novels are 'separate, unique individuals', who resist the urge to belong for fear of sacrificing their true selves, Vedanta offers a solution to this stalemate by drawing a distinction between the social self, which is defined by external action, and the essential self, which emerges only through conscious submission to the true reality. Thus is a further distinction implied, between the superficial reality, and the underlying reality; 'the aim of human life, we are told, is to realize the Atman, our essential nature, and hence our identity with the one, underlying Reality'.[45] Isherwood's belief performs, up to a point, the function of Waugh and Greene's Catholicism or of Warner and Upward's Marxism. It defines the individual by placing him in a wider context, by establishing his *connection* with an underlying reality. Catholicism and Communism, however, do so by defining the significance of external action, whereas Vedanta does so by denying its significance altogether. One achieves union with Brahman only through the full acceptance of the unimportance of action. The fear that 'Christopher' expresses in the first 'Berlin Diary', that his future life will be an accumulation of meaningless actions, becomes through Vedanta an acceptance of this state of affairs as eminently desirable:

> In general, mankind almost always acts with attachment: that is to say, with fear and desire. Desire for a certain result, and fear that this result will not be obtained. Attached action binds us to the world of appearance, to the continual doing of more action. We live in a delirium of doing, and the consequences of our past actions condition the actions we are about to perform. . . .
>
> But there is another way of performing action; and this is without fear and without desire. . . .
>
> All work becomes equally and vitally important . . . every action, under certain circumstances and for certain people, may be a stepping-stone to spiritual growth – if it is done in the spirit of non-attachment. All good and all evil is relative to the individual point of growth. For each individual, certain acts are absolutely wrong. Indeed, there may well be acts which are absolutely wrong for every individual alive on earth today. But, in the highest sense, there can be neither good nor evil.[46]

When Isherwood interprets Vedanta as denying, 'in the highest sense', the existence of good and evil, he is effectively throwing the full weight of a moral philosophy and religious belief behind the conclusions already implicit in *Goodbye to Berlin* and *Mr Norris Changes Trains*. The narrators of these novels are without systems or beliefs by which to define the worlds they observe – Bernhard Landauer or Mr Norris consequently remain enigmas for the narrators. Vedanta asserts that no such system exists, and no such definition is desirable. To define individuals by the rules of good and evil is to impose limitations upon their individuality. Isherwood suggests a resolution of the paradox in *Mr Norris Changes Trains* through Olga's 'exquisite fancy needlework'. Olga and her actions may be judged as good or evil, but her art, the product of her true self, is beyond moral evaluation. Vedanta supports this kind of resolution, for it maintains that true individuality, the 'essential self', emerges only when the urge to define and evaluate action has been completely conquered.

NOTES

1. *The Whispering Gallery* p. 181.
2. *Christopher and His Kind* p. 68.
3. Ibid p. 43.

4. Ibid p. 80.
5. Ibid p. 71.
6. *Mr Norris Changes Trains* p. 40.
7. *Goodbye to Berlin* p. 186.
8. Ibid pp.19–20.
9. *Mr Norris Changes Trains* pp. 76–7.
10. *The Auden Generation* p. 180.
11. *Nobody Talks Politics* (1936) p. 204.
12. *Goodbye to Berlin* p. 174.
13. Ibid p. 300.
14. *Christopher and His Kind* pp. 227–8.
15. 'Preface' *All the Conspirators* (1957) pp. 7–8.
16. Ibid.
17. *All the Conspirators* (1928) p. 93.
18. *World Within World* pp. 141–2.
19. Stanley Poss, 'Christopher Isherwood: A Conversation on Tape' *London Magazine* 1 (June 1961) p. 55.
20. Untitled preface to 'Evening at the Bay' *Exhumations* p. 173.
21. 'The Purpose of a Left Review' *Left Review* 1 (June 1935) pp. 364–5.
22. 'Magic and Materialism' *Left Review* 3 (February 1937) p. 33.
23. 'Fables and Reportage' *Left Review* 2 (November 1936) p. 782.
24. *Goodbye to Berlin* p. 215.
25. *Mr Norris Changes Trains* p. 11.
26. Ibid p. 49.
27. Ibid pp. 58–9.
28. Ibid pp. 204–5.
29. Ibid pp. 243–4.
30. Ibid p. 218.
31. Ibid p. 25.
32. Ibid p. 279.
33. Ibid pp. 122–3.
34. 'Review' (1938) *Essays 1* p. 334.
35. *Goodbye to Berlin* p. 13.
36. Ibid p. 267.
37. Ibid p. 22.
38. Ibid p. 14.
39. *Journey to a War* (1939) p. 196.
40. *Christopher and His Kind* p. 17.
41. Untitled preface to 'Vedanta and the West' *Exhumations* p. 97.
42. *An Approach to Vedanta* (Hollywood 1963) p. 10.
43. *My Guru and His Disciple* (1980) p. 49.
44. 'Introduction' *Vedanta for the Western World* (1948) p. 5.
45. Ibid p. 3.
46. 'The Gita and War' (1948) *Exhumations* pp. 109–10.

Chapter 7

George Orwell

Within his particular literary generation, George Orwell was something of an exception. He is regarded by many as the conscience of the thirties, the lone writer who, whilst deeply involved in the issues of the time, managed to keep his head when all about were losing theirs. For many of his contemporaries, Catholicism or Communism seemed to offer answers to the questions they were asking, yet Orwell was contemptuous of both. He subscribed to a notion of the decade dominated by the twin orthodoxies; the ordinary man was caught up in a struggle for the ownership of his soul. In essays and reviews, Orwell would ridicule the undefined mass or writers and intellectuals for the speed with which they were flocking towards Rome, and in greater numbers towards Moscow. While others saw these established beliefs as a means of reversing the trend towards social disorder and the suppression of the individual, Orwell took the opposite view. For him, Catholicism and Communism were certain to accelerate the process by which 'the autonomous individual is ceasing to exist'.[1] What other writers might have recognized as a problem of belief, Orwell saw as an insurmountable contradiction – as far as he was concerned, the decision to believe, far from being an assertion of individuality and independence, was in effect a renunciation of them.

Yet combined with this contempt for Catholicism and Communism, Orwell's writings reveal a deep sympathy for the motivations of the believer, the need in a confusing and chaotic world for 'something to believe in'.[2] His hopes for the future lay in the continued integrity of the individual as the fundamental component of any society. He was also aware that to rely on the self alone, and to disregard the world outside, was in the end destructive of the self: 'you can't ignore Hitler, Mussolini, unemployment, aeroplanes and the radio; you can only pretend to do so, which means lopping off a large chunk of your consciousness'.[3] He regarded the deliberate withdrawal from mundane concerns as leading not to an expansion and rarefaction of the sensibility, but to an inevitable contraction, and he damned that legion of writers, most but not all on the outer fringes of serious literature, who dared to ignore events in Europe: 'a novelist is not obliged to write directly about contemporary history, but a novelist who simply disregards the major public events of the moment is generally either a footler or a plain idiot'.[4] The problem then becomes to find a context for these events, a mode of explanation. Orwell does it is true sometimes speak as though the mere decision to face reality is enough in itself; only choose to write about 'contemporary history' and the choice will impose its own kind of order. In this respect, he was offering a sophisticated version of reportage, in which the artist had only to describe things as they are, through a style as clear as 'a window-pane',[5] and he would be describing reality as it truly and permanently exists. If the presence of a fundamental and unalterable reality may be assumed, then belief, which redefines the observable reality, is, in Orwell's terms, both superfluous and wrong. Alan Sandison has pointed to this faith of Orwell's in a natural world that exists outside the power of any system of belief to change it: 'As in other matters Orwell is quite fundamental in this: objective nature is real *not* illusory, verifiable by the senses and the senses alone. Only because nature exists objectively can our senses affirm themselves as organs of a personal self, which possesses, in consequence, the capacity to reach and sustain individual judgement, and asserts the freedom of the individual conscience.'[6] Ideally, independent self and objective reality mutually support each other's continued existence. But doubts about one can give rise to doubts about the other. Increasingly in the thirties, Orwell came to question the existence of an objective reality, and to question at the same time the concept of individuality which depends upon it.

In *Coming Up for Air*, the observable reality does change, beyond recognition, and with it goes the hero's understanding of himself. George Bowling has defined his individuality by his past, by past places and past events, and his confidence in his own significance depends upon his ability to prove that these places did exist, and that these events took place. His pilgrimage to his birthplace leads him to the realization that his understanding of himself is based upon a reality that no longer exists, and may indeed never have existed. He is, as a result, without any sure idea of himself, and in turn unable to cope with and understand reality as it now exists. The process is, in other words, a self-perpetuating one. The nature of reality changes, calling into question the individual's understanding of himself. This leads in turn to loss of faith in his own power to define reality. The world changes, as it was doing so rapidly in the nineteen-thirties, and the individual loses his bearings. The need to maintain bearings, to hold on to one's place in the world, is behind the sweeping generalizations Orwell frequently made. In his recurrent jibes at, for example, vegetarians or homosexuals or 'simple-lifers', he was often conscious of ignoring internal contradictions in order to arrive at a satisfying certainty. There is a revealing passage in a letter to Stephen Spender, in which he admits to this failure to account for the particular in his attitude to the general: 'You ask how it is that I attacked you not having met you, & on the other hand changed my mind after meeting you. . . . Even if when I met you I had not happened to like you, I should still have been bound to change my attitude, because when you meet anyone in the flesh you realize immediately that he is a human being and not a sort of caricature embodying certain ideas.'[7] Orwell's habit of defining people in black and white terms thus had a way of breaking down on acquaintance. His ability to compartmentalize and define the world in which he moved depended largely on being able to maintain the superficial view. The desire for certainty pushed him into extreme positions, giving rise to attitudes which sound uncomfortably close to bigotry and crankiness. The more easily to explain, he would deliberately overlook inconsistencies and contradictions.

He remained at the same time alive to these inconsistencies, and appreciated them for their own sake. It is this basic contradiction in Orwell's character which allowed him on the one hand to sympathize with a belief which offered a system for defining the world, and on the other prevented him from subscribing to such a belief because it seemed to him to threaten to impose uniformity. But this leads to yet another contradiction. Orwell's antagonism towards Catholicism and Communism was also rooted, at least in part, in what he saw as the assumption of superiority by a group from which he felt himself excluded. His resentment can be traced to his memories of himself as a schoolboy, ugly, smelly, and outcast, socially and physically unfit to be one of the gang of handsome, rugger-playing, fee-paying schoolfellows. Out of this early sense of isolation grew a deliberate alliance with all ordinary men against those who claimed to be, in some way, extraordinary. Orwell in the thirties made himself the spokesman of the heterosexual, meat-eating man, objecting to homosexuality or to vegetarianism, to Catholicism or to Communism, because they contained an implied insult to the ordinary way of life. Catholicism and Communism were available to all, but they remained, in England anyway, the preserve of the few. In *The Road to Wigan Pier*, Orwell makes clear that he considers the notions of the middle-class Communist to have next to no relevance to the lives of the working class, subject as they are to conditions which for the privileged intellectual are mere abstractions. Literary Communists were an exclusive band, out of touch with reality; Orwell felt himself to be living in that reality.

His attacks upon the literary left of the thirties are remarkable for their combination of apparent reasonableness with impossible generalization:

> The leading figures in this group are Auden, Spender, Day-Lewis, Mac-Neice, and there is a long string of writers of more or less the same tendency, Isherwood, John Lehmann, Arthur Calder-Marshall, Edward Upward, Alec Brown, Philip Henderson, and many others. . . . I am lumping them together simply according to tendency. Obviously there are very great variations in talent. But when one compares these writers with the Joyce-Eliot generation, the immediately striking thing is how much easier it is to form them into a group. Technically they are closer together, politically they are almost indistinguishable, and their criticisms of one another's work have always been (to put it mildly) good natured.[8]

Orwell is right to lump these writers 'together simply according to tendency', but he is implying at the same time that to distinguish amongst them at all would be, disregarding talent, an almost impossible task. They are defined as the 'pansy pinks' in large measure because Orwell *needs* to see them as comprising an homogeneous whole. His individuality as man and writer depends upon being able to describe other writers as forming the kind of non-differentiated mass that threatens his individuality. Considered separately, they are simply individuals like himself; *en masse*, they form a kind of reflector off which Orwell may bounce his own claims to uniqueness. Orwell's feeling of exclusion, from a group confident in its superiority, is even more specific in his objections to the Catholic Church as 'not so much a body of thought as . . . a kind of glorified family bank – a limited company paying enormous dividends, with non-members rigidly excluded from benefits'.[9] Orwell denies any claims Catholicism might have to intellectual seriousness, just as he dismissed the intellectual pretensions of literary Marxism. The satisfaction for the contemporary Catholic or Marxist springs in his view purely from belonging, from acquiring a spurious purpose. He coupled Catholics and Communists as 'the extremists at the opposite poles of thought',[10] covering by this rhetorical device all those who prey upon the uncertainty and insecurity of the modern man, luring him into complete subjection by a paradoxical appeal to this desire for significance. His particular vehemence towards Catholicism springs too from his middle-class inheritance, the conventional Protestant fear of unknown rites and papist conspiracies. His early writings contain numerous references to 'professional R.C.s', 'stinking R.C.s', and to the necessity of keepng the country safe from the R.C.s. The term 'R.C.', and Orwell's insistence on referring to Catholics always as Roman Catholics, confirm in themselves the conventional middle-class origins of his prejudice. He was in a way merely building upon and elaborating in the thirties a resentment he had absorbed from his upbringing, the threat to easy-going Protestant individuality apparently posed by the secret society of Catholics.

It would be misleading to imply an absolutely rigid correspondence between Orwell's antipathy towards Communism and his antipathy towards Catholicism, for the latter was reinforced by Orwell's automatic equation of the Church with reaction. This is a commonplace, and it would be perverse to call it an unjustified one. Orwell was especially galled to read, in the *Criterion* of January 1932, some remarks of T. S. Eliot on the servant problem, which he quoted in a letter to a friend. Eliot did not think much of having only one servant. 'I should prefer,' he wrote, 'to employ a large staff of servants, each doing much lighter work but profiting by the benefits of the cultured and devout atmosphere of the home in which they lived.'[11] This Orwell labelled the 'Anglo-Catholic standpoint', which for his purposes was indistinguishable from the Catholic. He was confirmed in his equation of religion and reaction by the events of the Spanish Civil War, in which they were officially united under Franco's Insurgents. He accepted the definition of religion-as-crutch, and saw it as an even less admirable attempt to come to terms with reality than Communism. Any left-wing political belief gave at the very least the appearance of being able to change the social reality for the better. Catholicism did not offer the means of altering reality, but preached instead a doctrine of acceptance. It was for Orwell a simple panacea for complex ills, a means of covering up what was wrong with the world rather than a true solution. He pursued his scepticism further, to regard conversion to Catholicism as a form of moral cowardice. 'One cannot', he noted of Evelyn Waugh, 'really be Catholic and grown-up.'[12] Conversion was the act of a child who could not 'face an adult world', a deliberate refusal to accept the insecurity of adulthood.

Orwell's rejection of Catholicism and Communism sprang in part from his own awareness of their attractions. He was able successfully to resist them by codifying both doctrines, turning them in his imagination into twin conspirators, plotting the takeover of the modern soul. On a less stylized level, however, Orwell's resistance to the attractions of exclusiveness and communal purpose was more vulnerable – his writings of the thirties reveal the very desire to 'belong' that he saw at the base of religious and political commitment.

Whether as a *plongeur* in Paris or a hop-picker in Kent, Orwell gains immense satisfaction from belonging temporarily to a definable group. Information about Paris hotels or the best method of picking hops is passed on to the uniformed reader with the authority of the insider. And when, in *Homage to Catalonia*, Orwell condemns the monolithic structure of a Communism blind to individuality, he does so from the vantage-point of one who belongs to a smaller, and therefore *more* exclusive and *more* definable group, the P.O.U.M. It seems indeed that part of the failure of Communism and Catholicism for Orwell lay in their spreading their nets too wide. These rather smaller groups, to which Orwell at various times belonged, have rules as rigid as any political or religious doctrine, and the intricacies of these rules are presented with relish. The difference is that the sense of communal purpose to be derived from such groups is a finite one – Orwell belonged, in the P.O.U.M. for example, to a group that was large enough to offer the individual purpose that comes from sharing a cause, yet not large enough to render the individual contribution insignificant. The function of these groups was not, like Communism or Catholicism, to provide a means of comprehending the world; they did offer however, something of what the two major beliefs provided Orwell's contemporaries, a bolstering of the individual position through common cause. Whether it be revolutionary comradeship, religious brotherhood, or simply the hop-pickers' *esprit de corps*, the effect is similar – the modern world remains very much outside, threatening and amorphous, but in the security of companionship and shared purpose, the individual feels more able to resist its encroachment.

Orwell retained throughout his work a consistent awareness of the importance of the real world, believing that an artistic point could only be made, or a moral only be drawn, by honestly reflecting it. To preach the moral outside a realistic context was to deprive the text of its imperative force. 'The truth is that the written word loses its power if it departs too far, or rather if it stays away too long, from the ordinary world where two and two make four.'[13] He believed that ideas should constantly be tested against reality, and that reality should not be made to conform, or assumed to conform, to an ideal. In Orwell's mind, the writer had a responsibility to face his situation, but that responsibility did not carry with it the right of didacticism. He did however believe himself to be working in the widest sense for a cause, particularly after the Spanish Civil War had focussed certain issues for him: 'Every line of serious work that I have written since

1930 has been written, directly or indirectly, *against* totalitarianism and *for* democratic Socialism, as I understand it.'[14] He assumed that, ideally, the best novelist would work by a sort of unconscious selection system so that the very structure and interaction of scenes in the book would suggest a political and moral attitude; the authorial view should be implied rather than imposed. The moral force of a novel will be the result of the author's working 'under a sense of compulsion, and not like an amateur cook following the instructions on a packet of Crestona cake-flour'.[15] Orwell's detachment is not then a clinical one; the novelist's involvement in the world he describes, his personal concern in the issues at stake, is an essential part of his ability to observe and judge.

In *A Clergyman's Daughter*, Dorothy Hare suffers the disillusionment of her generation, the realization that her wishy-washy Anglicanism is simply incapable of explaining and defining her existence. It is not an awareness of suffering on a large scale that precipitates Dorothy's dramatic loss of faith, but a sudden revulsion from all the petty horrors of life, from Mrs Pither's 'grey-veined, flaccid legs', and the 'dark, dewy moustache' on Miss Mayfill's upper lip. It is an awareness of mortality, for which religion offers no real consolation. Dorothy is, however, eventually struck by the knowledge that, inadequate as her faith had been, there seems little else: 'There was, she saw clearly, no possible substitute for faith, no pagan acceptance of life as sufficient to itself, no pantheistic cheer-up stuff, no pseudo-religion of 'progress' with visions of glittering utopiae and ant-heaps of steel and concrete. It is all or nothing. Either life on earth is a preparation for something greater and more lasting, or it is meaningless, dark and dreadful.'[16] The thirties predicament is effectively stated. Dorothy rejects any attempt to replace a lost faith, for she recognizes that religious faith can only exist within a society by unconscious agreement. Once it has gone, it cannot be re-imposed. She is unwilling, however, to reject the legacy of Anglicanism, the Protestant values of diligence and application, honesty and self-respect. These she hangs onto, despite the larger loss. Dorothy's final decision, to make the best of things, amounts to an assertion of instinctive, unfocussed faith; that despite all appearances to the contrary, there is a meaning and a purpose to life. Orwell shared this illogical optimism. In a letter to Geoffrey Gorer in 1939, he happily combined a reference to the horrors that were coming with an enthusiastic list of plans for the future. The world may be 'meaningless, dark and dreadful'; meanwhile one carries on, as Dorothy resolves to do, with 'what is customary, useful and acceptable'.

Dorothy Hare initially rejects her society and its values, but she returns to that society in the end, with a renewed if vaguely defined purpose. Gordon Comstock, in *Keep the Aspidistra Flying*, follows a parallel path, but his return to society and his renewed purpose are given symbolic weight. The 'money-god' which Gordon spends most of the novel trying to escape, is not very different from the superficial Anglicanism that causes Dorothy to flee. In both cases, the values of self-reliance and decency and hard work are shown to have survived the disappearance of the faith which justified them, and been increasingly corrupted into the self-perpetuating modern values of commercialism and self-serving pragmatism. These values, the rules by which modern society works, are symbolized by the aspidistra, which pursues Gordon relentlessly. The aspidistra is indestructible, and escape from it impossible. Society must be accepted as it exists, its oppressiveness confronted in an attempt to discover positive values within the apparently negative. Gordon does discover these positive values, more by an act of will than through any intellectual conviction:

The lower-middle-class people in there, behind their lace curtains, with their children and their scraps of furniture and their aspidistras – they lived by the money-code, sure enough, and yet they contrived to keep their decency. The money-code as they interpreted it was not merely cynical and hoggish. They had their standards, their inviolable points of honour. They 'kept themselves respectable' – kept the aspidistra flying. Besides, they were *alive*. They were bound up in the bundle of life. They begot children, which is what the saints and the soul-savers never by any chance do.
The aspidistra is the tree of life, he thought suddenly.[18]

The deification of the aspidistra is the corollary to Dorothy's half-articulated faith in the ordinary, everyday life. The aspidistra, a reflection of everything middle-class, becomes in Gordon's mind the embodiment of middle-class values and standards, themselves holding symbolically the power to evaluate action. The individual desire for significance leads directly to a kind of willed belief in 'standards' that cannot be convincingly defined. Gordon's sudden vision of the aspidistra as the 'tree of life' is the absurd result of a desperate need for belief, a need so profound that it creates the object of belief by an act of sheer will. *A Clergyman's Daughter* and *Keep the Aspidistra Flying* reveal an artistic dishonesty born of desperation. In no other thirties novel are the novelist's disillusionment and his need to believe in such stark opposition. They are cataloques of obsession and despair, resolved without regard to either logic or art.

This division exists in all Orwell's fiction, between the instinctive

conviction that reality is oppressive and threatening, and the contradictory conviction that within that reality may be discovered positive
values which will reconcile the individual to his environment, defining his function within it. This division, so described, recurs
throughout the fiction of the thirties generation, and is behind the
opposition of depressing reality and positive faith that can be seen in
Journey to the Border or *Brighton Rock*. In both these novels, the
established beliefs of Communism and Catholicism act as a kind of
intermediary between the two extremes, resolving to some extent at
least the tension between apparent opposites. Positive values are
extracted from the negative reality by the medium of belief, a belief
that offers to the believer a universal and unchallengeable authority.
The division is clearer and more irreconcilable in Orwell's fiction for
his refusal to accept such a belief. Instead the individual relies upon
his *own* power to resist the oppressive reality; he is aided in this only
by his conviction, empirically verifiable but impossible to 'prove', that
positive values *do* exist, and do retain an essential indestructibility.

Orwell's last novel of the thirties, *Coming Up for Air*, pursues more
rigorously this question of the relationship between individual and
the society he inhabits. George Bowling is caught in the predicament of the times; everywhere he turns he sees the threat posed
to his individual existence. Everything is 'slick and shiny and
streamlined';[19] the world is being rapidly covered by Mrs Beaver's
chromium plating. George keeps the outside world at bay by applying
the enemy's tactics of standardization and simplification. He resists
the uniformity of the modern world with a combination of anger and
wild generalization: 'I remembered a bit I'd read in the paper somewhere about these food-factories in Germany where everything's
made out of something else. Ersatz, they call it. . . . That's the way
we're going nowadays. Everything slick and streamlined, everything
made out of something else. Celluloid, rubber, chromium steel everywhere, arc lamps blazing all night, glass rooves over your head, radios
all playing the same tune, no vegetation left, everything cemented
over.'[20] As the world races of its own accord towards chaos, there is a
duty to resist, a duty which Orwell expressed in a letter to Cyril
Connolly in 1938. 'Everything one writes now is overshadowed by
this ghastly feeling that we are rushing towards a precipice and,
though we shan't actually prevent ourselves or anyone else from
going over, must put up some sort of fight.'[21] One may 'put up some
sort of fight' by confronting society, and establishing one's connections with what is left of the 'real' world, with those few patches
which have not yet been cemented over.

George Bowling becomes increasingly aware that this is the only possible course of action open to him. He realizes that he has no influence upon the world. The world exerts its influence on him and he has no say in the matter. As he believes that no action can alter the course of events, his instincts draw him to the past, to the memories of Edwardian security that retained their hold over the literary imagination in the thirties. George recognizes that it is a human failing to romanticize a past era, but the remembered world nevertheless retains its significance for him. George's pre-war existence established his self, and his post-war existence continuously undermines it. The logical conclusion in his eyes is to verify his past, to re-establish his connections with that world and thereby re-establish his self. The inevitable failure of his pilgrimage to Lower Binfield, his realization that his past is in effect unverifiable, implies in some fundamental way that George Bowling, individual, no longer exists. His final discovery that the pool in which he fished as a boy has become a rubbish dump recalls Anthony Last's realization that 'there is no City. Mrs Beaver has covered it with chromium plating and converted it into flats'. Anthony Last tells us what his time in the forest has taught him, and George Bowling tells us 'what his stay in Lower Binfield has taught him' – that '*it's all going to happen*. All the things you've got at the back of your mind, the things you're terrified of, the things that you tell yourself are just a nightmare or only happen in foreign countries.'[22]

The conclusion of *Coming Up for Air* is an apparent admission of defeat. The trend towards chaos is irreversible. He has rejected the illusory consolations of belief, of daily routine, of anger, of memories, and of a 'real' world beneath the modern, superficial reality. The final rejection is the most shattering for George, for it springs from the realization that a real world, as he understands it, simply does not exist. The nature of reality has changed, and the individual is powerless against it. At the same time the individual, in the person of George Bowling, does not quite succumb to the world he inhabits, for George retains his ability to see what is happening. Like the narrators of Isherwood's Berlin novels, he cannot finally cope with the reality he describes, but neither does he succumb to it. William Bradshaw and 'Christopher Isherwood' are able to avoid sinking into the chaos of Berlin because they have the power to return to England. Orwell in *Down and Out in Paris and London*, 'Hop-Picking in Kent', *The Road to Wigan Pier*, and *Homage to Catalonia* has a similar power. But his hero George Bowling does not. He is permanently implicated in the fate he foresees for his society. The narrator accepts that he is *of* the world he describes. The only power he retains is the power to record.

NOTES

1. 'Literature and Totalitarianism' (1941) *Essays 2* p. 134.
2. 'Inside the Whale' p. 515.
3. 'Review' (1936) *Essays 1* p. 249.
4. 'Inside the Whale' p. 494.
5. 'Why I Write' p. 7.
6. *The Last Man in Europe* (1974) pp. 22–3.
7. 'Letter to Stephen Spender' (15? April 1938) *Essays 1* p. 313.
8. 'Inside the Whale' p. 511.
9. 'Review' (1932) p. 80.
10. 'Review' (1936) p. 257.
11. Quoted in 'Letter to Brenda Salkeld (extract)' (7 March 1935) *Essays 1* p. 151.
12. 'Extracts from a Manuscript Notebook' (1949) *Essays 4* p. 513.
13. 'Review' (1936) *Essays 1* p. 231.
14. 'Why I Write' p. 5.
15. 'Review' (1936) p. 247.
16. *A Clergyman's Daughter* (1935) p. 313.
17. 'Letter to Geoffrey Gorer' (20 January 1939) *Essays 1* p. 382.
18. *Keep the Aspidistra Flying* (1936) p. 308.
19. *Coming Up for Air* p. 31.
20. Ibid pp. 32–3.
21. 'Letter to Cyril Connolly' (14 December 1938) *Essays 1* p. 362.
22. *Coming Up for Air* p. 274.

Chapter 8

Summing Up

In an interview he gave in the mid-nineteen-sixties, Christopher Isherwood reflected upon his successful post-war career in the United States. 'I have always,' he said, 'challenged the idea that writers have to have roots in the conventional sense.'[1] His words refer most directly to the dramatic break of 1939, when he and Auden made the decision to go to America; but they hark back too to an earlier time, to Isherwood as he was throughout the nineteen-thirties, Isherwood the wanderer, the observer, the outsider, making his notes before moving on to somewhere else. He implies, by this questioning of the artist's relationship to his past, a characteristically modern notion of the artist as stateless, as one who is able and indeed obliged to cross borders and frontiers, who sees the right to travel and to change one's base as part of the artist's right to his material, his right to perspective. Isherwood, and others of his generation, saw themselves in the thirties as having to transcend the limitations of their own society and upbringing. Accordingly, they moved about a good deal, so that travel became something of a way of life for the thirties generation. Not only to the countries of Western Europe, but as far afield as China and Africa and South America. 'For myself and many better than me,' Waugh began sententiously, 'there is a fascination in the distant and barbarous, and particularly in the borderlands of conflicting cultures and states of development, where ideas, uprooted from their traditions, become oddly changed in transplantation. It is there that I find the experience vivid enough to demand translation into literary form.'[2] Waugh's justification of the urge to travel is curiously elusive. He presents it as on the one hand a search for intellectual stimulus, a journey through the realm of 'ideas'. On the other hand, it is seen as providing something more basic, something closely akin to old-fashioned inspiration. But most revealing of all is the emphasis not upon the foreign custom or the foreign idea, but upon a kind of middle ground, 'the borderlands of conflicting cultures and states of development', lying somewhere between home and abroad, between received and new ideas, between the familiar and the mysterious. It was this borderland, this half-way territory, that captured the interest of thirties writers. The title of Upward's novel, *Journey to the Border*, containing as it does a characteristic thirties motif, also contains the real destination. For what lay over the border, the foreign country and the foreign state of mind, was to remain throughout the thirties vague and undescribed, whilst the full force of the writer's attention was concentrated on the frontier. Waugh's novels of the thirties which are set wholly or in part in exotic lands – *Black Mischief, A Handful of Dust, Scoop* – yet reveal no serious interest in them. No attempt is made to understand the foreign point or view, beyond the fact that it is foreign and different. These distant and barbarous places are there for contrast; despite the foreign settings, the real focus of the novels is upon the old, 'civilized' values, the ideas and attitudes embodied in the English characters, and the ways in which these values stand up to the experience of disorientation. The effect of being confronted with other ways of life, in which priorities are different, is not to stimulate in the traveller – Tony Last, for example, or Basil Seal – a new and coherent system with which to cope with new experience. Instead the hero is thrown back upon the old values, upon a threadbare code of gentlemanly conduct. To travel is, to adopt once more Isherwood's terminology from *Lions and Shadows*, a kind of test – a test of the individual, and by implication of the society which created him. Waugh's thirties heroes, notably Tony Last in *A Handful of Dust*, end by failing this test rather badly.

The effect of the foreign and disorientating experience was to confirm, sometimes to the edge of parody, the Englishness of the fictional hero. George in *The Wild Goose Chase*, the tutor in *Journey to the Border*, Isherwood's narrators in the Berlin novels, remain at the end of it all strangely untouched by the depths they have apparently peered into; there is a chilling complacency about them. The un-doubted quality of the Berlin novels is often attributed, in a casual way, to the vivid picture they paint of the foreign country, and to the first hand insight they provide into the early growth of Nazism. And yet the Berlin novels do not do that at all. If one were after a clearer understanding of the Fascist mentality; of the way in which a political phenomenon took hold, of its insidious power to corrupt, of its hold over ordinary people; if one were, in short, after an insight into Fascism, then *Mr Norris Changes Trains* and *Goodbye to Berlin* are not the places to look. Instead they offer a different kind of understanding – of what it is like to be caught up in the incomprehensible, to be faced with a society which is based upon dynamics that one simply does not understand. Even the phrase 'caught up' is misleading, for Isher-wood's English narrators, William Bradshaw and 'Christopher Isher-wood', are not seriously caught up at all. They have the power to leave, and in the end they do leave, rejecting explanation and involvement in favour of moving on. The central interest throughout is the English narrator, and what happens to his complacency and self-interest when he is up against the inexplicable. Neither narrator is profoundly affected by the Berlin experience. It precipitates no serious crisis of conscience. Instead they come away puzzled and disturbed, with little to fall back on but the shaky supports of detachment and reserve.

To some extent, what is true of the heroes of the Berlin novels is also true of Isherwood himself. For Isherwood as for his contemporaries, 'abroad' was a gigantic mirror in which he gazed at his own preoccupations; there were few attempts to put personal preoccupations aside in order to explore the preoccupations of others, even if only for the purposes of comparison. The broad concerns of Warner and Upward, for example, with discovering the appropriate fictional form to reflect the necessity of political commitment, were shared by novelists in the Soviet Union and the United States, in Germany and Scandinavia and elsewhere. Yet beyond a certain superficial debt to Kafka, their works are remarkably free of foreign influences. In terms of their stature as novelists, this is neither here nor there, but it does sit rather awkwardly with the professed internationalism of their political sympathies. In the cases of Waugh and Greene – both of whom were practising Catholics throughout the thirties – it might seem likely that the position of writers in Catholic countries such as France and Spain and Italy, the problems they faced and the means by which they dealt with them, would be a subject of particular interest. Broadly speaking, this was not the case, although in postwar years Graham Greene has increasingly turned his attention outwards, to consider the work of other writers in other countries. By way of contrast, there is an anecdote in Christopher Sykes's biography of Waugh in which the author recalls a meeting he arranged in Paris in 1949 between Waugh and Paul Claudel. As Sykes remembers, 'Evelyn was so shy of speaking French to a French master, and so fearful of not understanding what was said to him, that he feigned total ignorance of the language,'[3] so that the two distinguished Catholic writers were obliged to communicate through the interpretation of Claudel's son and daughter-in-law. The meeting was not a success. It was essentially a clash of cultures, against which a shared commitment to religion and to literature seemed relatively insignificant.

Anecdotes do not prove anything, and of course Waugh is an extreme case, a man whose contempt for things foreign became increasingly in his later years just one more element in an elaborate personality. Nevertheless, when Isherwood questions the writer's need for 'roots in the conventional sense', he is glossing over something that is as true of himself, of Greene and Upward and Warner and Orwell, as it is in a vastly more theatrical and parodic way, of Waugh – that their roots were, and have remained, irrevocably English. Not merely English, but public school, Oxbridge, vintage 1905 or thereabouts. Far from dissociating themselves from their upbringing, these writers displayed an exaggerated consciousness of origins, which led in the thirties to a central and crucial paradox; the recognition of the inadequacy in the modern world of values inherited from another age, was coupled with an instinctive faith in those values – the values, in short, of the English gentleman – that prevented their complete abandonment. For me, one of the most moving emblems of the thirties is a photograph of himself which Waugh bravely included as the frontispiece to his travel-book, *Ninety-two Days*. He is dressed as though for a costume party, in genuine nineteenth-century explorer's rig. In his drill shorts, leggings, and bush hat, his right arm weighed down by an out-size, heavy-duty watch, he stares at a point beyond the range of the camera, a resigned and bewildered expression on his face. He is an Imperialist without an Empire, an explorer who is not sure which direction he is heading in, or indeed quite why he began the journey in the first place.

Yet such self-depreciation can also be a form of complacency. In *Journey to a War*, for example, Isherwood describes the strange antics of the travelling Englishman:

The stewards hurried up and down the corridor with hot face towels, bowls of rice, cups of tea. As the journey progressed, the tea grew nastier, tasting increasingly of fish. The two armed guards in the corridor – one of them surely not more than twelve years old – peered into our compartment to watch the foreign devils screaming with laughter at mysterious jokes, singing in high falsetto or mock operatic voices, swaying rhythmically backwards and forwards in their seats, reading aloud to each other from small crimson-bound books. The swaying was an exercise which we had invented, in a vain attempt to ward off constipation; the books were *Framley Parsonage* and *Guy Mannering*.[4]

The self-mockery is also self-congratulation. Auden and Isherwood, two travellers passing through a country and a culture they can never really understand, take refuge in their common background, in a whole network of jokes and references that protects them from whatever is outside. They may, as Isherwood goes on to say, find Trollope's England 'dull', but the very act of reading him, in an

enclosed compartment in the middle of China, amounts to an assertion of personal identity, a declaration that Auden and Isherwood
possess characters and habits of mind that are as incomprehensible to
the Chinese as the Chinese are to them.

To assert one's Englishness and thereby one's identity was something; but as so much of the thirties fiction makes clear, it was not of
itself enough. With chaos all around, only belief offered the final,
necessary support. Ironically, for a generation of writers to whom the
world through which they travelled was uncongenial and often
threatening, the beliefs they were attracted to were themselves 'foreign' in origin, regarded by others of their age and class as essentially
alien to an English way of life. But for these writers, to declare oneself
a Catholic or a Marxist was not, as might be expected, to declare
oneself an alien, a kind of honorary foreigner. Instead it strengthened
the individual's confidence in himself and his Englishness. Marxism
and Catholicism were in effect Anglicized, so that in examining the
Marxism of Upward and Warner, or the Catholicism of Greene and
Waugh, it is very often difficult to see more than the most tenuous
connections between these beliefs as they saw them, and these same
beliefs as they were subscribed to by other people in other countries.
When following the travels of Greene and Waugh through Catholic
countries, the dominant impression is not one of Catholic experiencing a sense of fellowship with other believers. It is of a lone sceptic,
who happens also to be a Catholic, observing and recording from a
position of detachment. For a belief, such as Catholicism, that was in
theory potentially applicable to every individual on earth, paradoxically owed a good deal of its power and attraction to the fact that it
was, in England at least, the province of the few. Greene's and
Waugh's Catholicism, and for that matter Isherwood's Vedanta, are
seen by the believers not as vast edifices, but as small corners of faith
in an irreligious world.

The thirties novelists were very conscious of themselves as standing against the forces of barbarism, and their beliefs helped them to
make that stand. In *Brideshead Revisited*, Waugh describes at the end of
the novel how Catholicism survives as a lone sanctuary flame, inex-
tinguishable but virtually unregarded by all but a small band of the
faithful. In *An Approach to Vedanta*, Isherwood relates how the philosophy, in which 'only one man in ten thousand would take an
interest',[5] was kept alive in Los Angeles in the forties by a handful of
believers, while across the Atlantic a civilization was being destroyed.
Part of the solace of belief actually derived from the size of congregation; one belonged to the small group of believers who saw truly. The

revolutionary socialism of Upward and Warner is also presented as claiming the allegiance of the few, for against the heroes of their fiction are posed vast and malignant worlds, inhabited by barbarians. At the end of *Journey to the Border*, the tutor's decision to ally himself with 'the way of the workers', is, despite the apparent suggestion of vast numbers in that phrase, in effect a decision to join the minority against the majority. The attractions of exclusiveness, of belonging to a group whose members share certain values and obey certain rules, may also be seen in Waugh's attitude to the aristocracy, in Isherwood's to homosexuality, or in Orwell's enthusiastic adoption of the role of hop-picker or down-and-out. But Catholicism and Marxism offered more than the refuge of a social sub-group. They offered a system which explained everything, which was universally applicable. At the same time, the aspects of these beliefs which emphasized the individual's similarity to everyone else – his equality in the sight of God, his duty as a soldier for the revolution – were subsequently underplayed, in favour of emphasizing the importance of the individual contribution to the cause. When Greene's whisky priest in *The Power and the Glory* assures his illegitimate daughter that she is so 'important', he is asserting what was for these novelists a fundamental function of the faith – its power to uphold the individual's confidence in his own distinctiveness and worth.

The thirties are characterized now as an age of belief. It is a sceptic's phrase, applied with hindsight by those who are sadder and wiser. It is a phrase which implies a corollary, a succeeding age of disillusionment, from which we look back at the naivety of earlier days. As such phrases go, it is accurate enough, but it also over-simplifies. People do not as a rule move clearly and sharply from idealism to scepticism, from belief to disillusionment. It might be more accurate to say that the two states exist simultaneously, engaged in a continuing battle for the upper hand. Naive idealism is only one aspect of the thirties. The jaundiced view is equally characteristic of the decade, and in some ways more so. Waugh and Greene in particular set the tone in the thirties for a sophisticated world-weariness that has profoundly influenced English prose ever since. This world-weariness has its own logic, for it sprang out of a generation whose members had been, as it were, born disillusioned, and for whom belief came only later. When it did come, it did not entirely supplant a native scepticism, but had to be accommodated to it. A reason why religious belief – Waugh and Greene's Catholicism, Isherwood's Vedanta – survived the thirties while political commitment as a rule did not, is that religious beliefs more easily allowed scepticism and faith to co-exist. Once adopted, the religious belief could be left almost out of sight, occasionally making its presence felt, but for the most part remaining in the background, a safety net against despair. Political belief on the other hand claimed the foreground, limiting the novelists' options in ways which finally defeated them. It is not that fiction and belief are, in the way of things, incompatible, but that novelists of the thirties were sometimes tempted in their work to offer simple solutions to complex problems. The novels which now seem truer to the thirties, and to the problems of embarking, not altogether willingly, on the twentieth century, are those which reveal a readiness to confront the sheer difficulty of it all.

NOTES

1. George Wickes, 'An Interview with Christopher Isherwood', *Shenandoah* 16 (ii, 1965) p. 35.
2. *Ninety-two Days*, pp. 13–14.
3. *Evelyn Waugh*, p. 331.
4. *Journey to a War*, pp. 47–8.
5. *An Approach to Vedanta*, p. 17.

Acknowledgements

Acknowledgements are due to the following for permission to quote from copyright material.

W. H. Auden: Extract from 'Spain 1937' in *The English Auden: Poems, Essays and Dramatic Writings, 1927–1939* (edited by Edward Mendelson). By permission of Faber & Faber Ltd., and Random House, Inc.

Bernard Bergonzi: Extract from *Reading the Thirties*. © 1978 by Bernard Bergonzi. By permission of Macmillan Ltd., and the University of Pittsburgh Press.

Cyril Connolly: Extract from 'Some Memories' in *W. H. Auden: A Tribute* (edited by Stephen Spender). By permission of George Weidenfeld & Nicolson Ltd. Extracts from *The Condemned Playground*. By permission of Deborah Rogers Ltd.

Fr. Martin D'Arcy: Extract from 'The Religion of Evelyn Waugh', in *Evelyn Waugh and His World* (edited by David Pryce-Jones). By permission of George Weidenfeld & Nicolson Ltd.

Christopher Dawson: Extract from *Religion and the Modern State*. By permission of Sheed & Ward Ltd.

Lewis Grassic Gibbon: Extracts from *Grey Granite*. By permission of Hutchinson Publ. Group Ltd.

Graham Greene: Extracts from *A Sort of Life, The Lawless Roads, The Name of Action, Rumour at Nightfall, It's a Battlefield, England Made Me, Journey without Maps, Brighton Rock*, and *The Power and the Glory*. By permission of Laurence Pollinger Ltd., and Viking Penguin Inc. Extracts from *Collected Essays*. By permission of The Bodley Head Ltd.

Aldous Huxley: Extract from *Eyeless in Gaza*. By permission of Mrs Laura Huxley, Chatto & Windus Ltd., and Harper & Row, Inc.

Samuel Hynes: Extract from *The Auden Generation*. By permission of The Bodley Head Ltd., and Viking Penguin Inc.

Christopher Isherwood: Extracts from *Exhumations*. By permission of Methuen & Co. Ltd., and Candida Donadio Assoc. Extracts from *Christopher and His Kind*. By permission of Eyre Methuen, and Farrar, Straus & Giroux, Inc. Extracts from *All The Conspirators*. Copyright 1928, 1957 by Christopher Isherwood. By permission of Jonathan Cape Ltd., and Candida Donadio Assoc. Extracts from *Mr. Norris Changes Trains*. By permission of Curtis Brown Ltd., and Candida Donadio Assoc. Extracts from *Goodbye to Berlin*. By permission of The Hogarth Press and Candida Donadio Assoc. Both stories were published in the United States in *The Berlin Stories* (New Directions). Copyright 1935 by Christopher Isherwood. Extracts from *Lions and Shadows*. Copyright 1947 by New Directions, copyright renewed 1977 by Christopher Isherwood. By permission of Associated Book Publishers Ltd., and Candida Donadio Assoc. Extracts from *Vedanta for the Western World*. By permission of George Allen & Unwin Ltd.

Wyndham Lewis: Extract from *Doom of Youth*. © Estate of the late Mrs G. A. Wyndham Lewis, by permission of the Wyndham Lewis Memorial Trust.

Louis MacNeice: Extract from *The Strings Are False* (Faber/OUP New York). By permission of David Higham Assoc. Ltd., and Oxford University Press, New York.

Dmitri Mirsky: Extract from *The Intelligentsia of Great Britain* (trans. by Alec Brown). By permission of Victor Gollancz Ltd.

George Orwell: Extracts from *A Clergyman's Daughter, Keep the Aspidistra Flying, The Road to Wigan Pier*, and *Coming Up For Air* (Gollancz). Extracts from *The Collected Essays, Journalism, and Letters of George Orwell* (Secker & Warburg). By permission of A. M. Heath & Co. Ltd., on behalf of the late Mrs. Sonia Brownell Orwell.

William Plomer: Extract from *At Home*. By permission of Jonathan Cape Ltd., on behalf of the Estate of William Plomer.

Alan Sandison: From *The Last Man in Europe*. By permission of Macmillan Ltd

Stephen Spender: Extract from *The Destructive Element*. By permission of Jonathan Cape Ltd., for the author. Extracts from *World Within World*. By permission of A. D. Peters & Co. Ltd., and Random House Inc.

Julian Symons: From *The Thirties*. By permission of Curtis Brown Ltd.

Edward Upward: Extract from 'Sketch for a Marxist Interpretation of Literature', in *The Mind in Chains* (edited by C. Day Lewis). By permission of Frederick Muller Ltd. Extracts from *The Railway Accident and other stories; Journey to the Border*; and, *In the Thirties*. By permission of William Heinemann Ltd.

Rex Warner: Extracts from *The Wild Goose Chase* and *The Professor*. Reprinted by permission of the author. Extracts from *The Cult of Power*. By permission of The Bodley Head Ltd. Extract from 'Education' in, *The Mind in Chains* (edited by C. Day Lewis). By permission of Frederick Muller Ltd.

Evelyn Waugh: Extract from an unpublished manuscript entitled 'An Open Letter to H. E. the Cardinal Archbishop of Westminster'. By permission of The Humanities Research Centre, The University of Texas at Austin, owners of the original manuscript, and by permission of A. D. Peters & Co. Ltd. Extracts from *Labels*. By permission of Duckworth & Co. Ltd. Extracts from *Decline and Fall, Vile Bodies, Black Mischief, A Handful of Dust, Mr. Loveday's Little Outing and Other Sad Stories*, and *Brideshead Revisited* (Chapman & Hall/Little Brown). By permission of A. D. Peters & Co. Ltd., and Little, Brown & Co. Extracts from *Robbery Under Law* (Chapman & Hall), *Remote People* and *Ninety Two Days* (both Duckworth), and extract from 'Come Inside', in *The Road to Damascus* (ed. J. A. O'Brien, W. H. Allen 1949). By permission of A. D. Peters & Co. Ltd.

Index